HIRAGANA

	a	i	u	e	o
a	あ	い	う	え	お
k	か (ka)	き (ki)	く (ku)	け (ke)	こ (ko)
s	さ (sa)	し (shi)	す (su)	せ (se)	そ (so)
t	た (ta)	ち (chi)	つ (tsu)	て (te)	と (to)
n	な (na)	に (ni)	ぬ (nu)	ね (ne)	の (no)
h	は (ha)	ひ (hi)	ふ (fu)	へ (he)	ほ (ho)
m	ま (ma)	み (mi)	む (mu)	め (me)	も (mo)
y	や (ya)		ゆ (yu)		よ (yo)
r	ら (ra)	り (ri)	る (ru)	れ (re)	ろ (ro)
w	わ (wa)				を (o)
n	ん (n)				

kya	kyu	kyo
きゃ	きゅ	きょ
sha	shu	sho
しゃ	しゅ	しょ
cha	chu	cho
ちゃ	ちゅ	ちょ
nya	nyu	nyo
にゃ	にゅ	にょ
hya	hyu	hyo
ひゃ	ひゅ	ひょ
mya	myu	myo
みゃ	みゅ	みょ

rya	ryu	ryo
りゃ	りゅ	りょ

	a	i	u	e	o
g	が (ga)	ぎ (gi)	ぐ (gu)	げ (ge)	ご (go)
z	ざ (za)	じ (ji)	ず (zu)	ぜ (ze)	ぞ (zo)
d	だ (da)	ぢ (ji)	づ (zu)	で (de)	ど (do)
b	ば (ba)	び (bi)	ぶ (bu)	べ (be)	ぼ (bo)
p	ぱ (pa)	ぴ (pi)	ぷ (pu)	ぺ (pe)	ぽ (po)

gya	gyu	gyo
ぎゃ	ぎゅ	ぎょ
ja	ju	jo
じゃ	じゅ	じょ

bya	byu	byo
びゃ	びゅ	びょ
pya	pyu	pyo
ぴゃ	ぴゅ	ぴょ

KATAKANA

	a	i	u	e	o
a	ア	イ	ウ	エ	オ
k	カ (ka)	キ (ki)	ク (ku)	ケ (ke)	コ (ko)
s	サ (sa)	シ (shi)	ス (su)	セ (se)	ソ (so)
t	タ (ta)	チ (chi)	ツ (tsu)	テ (te)	ト (to)
n	ナ (na)	ニ (ni)	ヌ (nu)	ネ (ne)	ノ (no)
h	ハ (ha)	ヒ (hi)	フ (fu)	ヘ (he)	ホ (ho)
m	マ (ma)	ミ (mi)	ム (mu)	メ (me)	モ (mo)
y	ヤ (ya)		ユ (yu)		ヨ (yo)
r	ラ (ra)	リ (ri)	ル (ru)	レ (re)	ロ (ro)
w	ワ (wa)				ヲ (o)
n	ン (n)				

kya	kyu	kyo
キャ	キュ	キョ
sha	shu	sho
シャ	シュ	ショ
cha	chu	cho
チャ	チュ	チョ
nya	nyu	nyo
ニャ	ニュ	ニョ
hya	hyu	hyo
ヒャ	ヒュ	ヒョ
mya	myu	myo
ミャ	ミュ	ミョ

rya	ryu	ryo
リャ	リュ	リョ

	ga	gi	gu	ge	go
g	ガ	ギ	グ	ゲ	ゴ
z	ザ (za)	ジ (ji)	ズ (zu)	ゼ (ze)	ゾ (zo)
d	ダ (da)	ヂ (ji)	ヅ (zu)	デ (de)	ド (do)
b	バ (ba)	ビ (bi)	ブ (bu)	ベ (be)	ボ (bo)
p	パ (pa)	ピ (pi)	プ (pu)	ペ (pe)	ポ (po)

gya	gyu	gyo
ギャ	ギュ	ギョ
ja	ju	jo
ジャ	ジュ	ジョ

bya	byu	byo
ビャ	ビュ	ビョ
pya	pyu	pyo
ピャ	ピュ	ピョ

色
Iro
Colors

赤 (い)* aka(i)*
red

青 (い)* ao(i)*
blue

黄色 (い)* kiiro(i)*
yellow

黒 (い)* kuro(i)*
black

白 (い)* shiro(i)*
white

緑 midori
green

オレンジ orenji
orange

ピンク pinku
pink

黄緑 kimidori
yellow-green

紺 kon
dark blue

水色 mizuiro
light blue

紫 murasaki
purple

茶色 / ブラウン
chairo / buraun
brown

灰色 / グレー
haiiro / gurē
gray

日本料理
Nihon ryōri
Japanese Food

すき焼き sukiyaki
beef and vegetables cooked in
sweet-salty soy sauce

しゃぶしゃぶ shabu shabu
Japanese variant of hot pot

焼肉 yakiniku
grilled meat

焼き鳥 yakitori
grilled chicken skewers

刺身 sashimi
raw fish

天ぷら tempura
deep-fried vegetables or seafood

から揚げ karaage
fried chicken

しょうが焼き shōgayaki
pork fried with ginger

鶏の照り焼き tori no teriyaki
chicken teriyaki

肉じゃが nikujaga
meat and potato stew

おでん oden
broth with egg, steamed fish
cake etc.

親子丼　oyako don
chicken and egg rice bowl

牛丼　gyū don
beef rice bowl

かつ丼　katsu don
pork cutlet rice bowl

天丼　ten don
tempura rice bowl

にぎりずし　nigiri zushi
sushi

ちらしずし　chirashi zushi
sashimi or various toppings
on sushi rice

いなりずし　inari zushi
sushi rice-stuffed fried tofu

のり巻き　norimaki
sushi roll

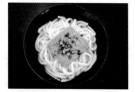

きつねうどん　kitsune udon
thick white wheat noodles
with deep-fried tofu

たぬきうどん　tanuki udon
thick white wheat noodles
with tempura batter

天ぷらそば　tempura soba
buckwheat noodles with tempura

ざるそば　zaru soba
cold soba with dipping sauce

しょうゆラーメン　shōyu rāmen
soy sauce based ramen

塩ラーメン　shio rāmen
salt based ramen

味噌ラーメン　miso rāmen
miso based ramen

とんこつラーメン　tonkotsu rāmen
pork bone based ramen

焼きそば　yakisoba
fried noodles

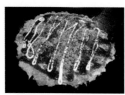

お好み焼き　okonomiyaki
Japanese pan-fried pizza
with various ingredients

もんじゃ焼き　monjayaki
thin Japanese pan-fried pizza
with various ingredients

たこ焼き　takoyaki
octopus dumpling

冷奴　hiyayakko
cold tofu

揚げ出し豆腐　agedashi dōfu
deep-fried tofu with broth

枝豆　edamame
boiled soybeans

卵焼き　tamagoyaki
fried rolled egg

おにぎり　onigiri
rice ball

お茶漬け　ochazuke
rice bowl filled with green tea

味噌汁　misoshiru
miso soup

とん汁　tonjiru
pork miso soup with vegetables

洋食
Yōshoku
Japanese Style
Western Food

コロッケ　korokke
croquette

えびフライ　ebifurai
fried shrimp

トンカツ　tonkatsu
pork cutlet

ハンバーグ　hambāgu
hamburger meat

カレーライス　karē raisu
curry with rice

カツカレー　katsu karē
pork cutlet curry

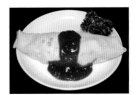

オムライス　omuraisu
fried omelette stuffed with rice

ミートソース　mīto sōsu
spaghetti meat sauce

中華料理
Chūka ryōri
Chinese Food

チャーハン　chāhan
fried rice

餃子　gyōza
pot stickers

春巻き　harumaki
spring roll

シュウマイ　shūmai
steamed meat dumpling

デザート
Dezāto
Desserts

ショートケーキ　shōtokēki
strawberry shortcake

シュークリーム　shūkurīmu
cream puff

漬物
Tsukemono
Pickled Vegetables

梅干　umeboshi
pickled plum

たくあん　takuan
pickled daikon radish

ふくじんづけ fukujinzuke
pickled vegetables in soy sauce

らっきょう rakkyō
Japanese leek pickles

キムチ kimuchi
Korean style pickles

薬味
Yakumi
Condiments

のり nori
nori seaweed

青のり aonori
green nori seaweed

かつおぶし katsuobushi
sliced dried bonito

紅しょうが beni shōga
pickled ginger

ごま goma
sesame

ねぎ negi
green onion

大根おろし daikon oroshi
grated daikon radish

七味 (とうがらし)
shichimi (tōgarashi)
a mixture of red pepper and other spices

わさび wasabi
wasabi

からし karashi
mustard

その他の食材
Sonota no shokuzai
Other Foods

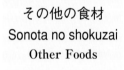

納豆 nattō
fermented soybeans

豆腐 tōfu
tofu

油揚げ abura age
deep-fried tofu

かまぼこ kamaboko
steamed fish cake

こんにゃく konnyaku
konjac potato gel

わかめ wakame
wakame seaweed

こんぶ kombu
kombu seaweed

たらこ tarako
salted cod roe

明太子 mentaiko
spiced cod roe

ask
PUBLISHING

NIHONGO
FUN & EASY

Survival Japanese Conversation
for Beginners

緒方 由希子
OGATA Yukiko

角谷 佳奈
SUMITANI Kana

左 弥寿子
HIDARI Yasuko

渡部 由紀子
WATANABE Yukiko

To Users of This Book

The idea to make this book came after we failed to come across a beginner-level text that met the needs of students hoping to learn practical Japanese for immediate use in the real world as opposed to grammar.

The majority of beginner texts we found made it difficult to grasp the Japanese language in a systematic way. Over-technical explanations, unnatural example sentences, and limited scope for a lesser learning experience, as well as choppy sentences that did not adequately portray an actual conversation, made it practically impossible to find a textbook that we felt would satisfy the curiosity of the adult learner.

This text is characterized by the following four points:

1. Instead of grammar, phrases and their function within a conversation are written out to help students learn natural sounding Japanese.
2. Units are composed of several different elements, with a variety of situations, functions, and topics to allow students to effectively learn genuinely helpful expressions in accordance with their interests.
3. Conversation drills are presented separately from grammatical explanations to help students easily understand both practical exercises and the workings of the Japanese language.
4. Each unit contains a variety of practice exercises to help students naturally acquire target phrases and expressions.

Our goal in creating this book was to realize a text that 1) motivated students to talk about a variety of subjects with sentence patterns they had just learned; 2) spoke to adults with a sense of intellectual curiosity in a practical way; and 3) made readers feel more familiar with Japan.

At the core of this book is our desire for everyone who has had the opportunity to come to Japan to enjoy their stay in the country. Nothing would make us happier than to know that this book in some way contributed to your having a positive experience in Japan.

Numerous people have contributed to the completion of this book since we first began writing it in 2007.

Our editor, Maiko Kohno, and illustrator, Noriaki Hiratsuka, went to great lengths to introduce us to the unknown world of publishing, and by far provided the greatest help in finishing this project.

Steve King of Pearson Education, who worked as our advisor, provided valuable insight wherever necessary. Matthew Harvey, husband of co-author Yukiko Watanabe, was always on hand to share ideas and lend his support right from the conceptual stages of the book. We would like to take this space to thank them again.

In closing, we would also like to offer our respect and gratitude to the following people at Iidabashi Japanese Language School: to the faculty, who provided feedback from their vast experience in using different teaching materials; to the staff, who took on additional tasks in their day-to-day workload to support the writing of this book from behind the scenes; and to all the students we have encountered in both the past and present, who have always been there to provide the motivation and inspiration to produce materials for learning Japanese. Thank you all from the bottom of our hearts.

The Authors

この本を使う方へ

　私たちがこのテキストを作ろうと思ったきっかけは、ビギナーレベルで、文法ではなく街ですぐに使える実践的な日本語を学びたい、という学習者に「これ！」と勧められるテキストになかなか出会えなかったからです。既存のテキストは文法の積み上げを意識しすぎて、日本語が非常に不自然だったり、場面に特化しすぎて学習内容に広がりがなかったり、また、文法が細切れに出てくるため、「日本語」を体系的にとらえるのが難しいように感じました。そのため、これでは学習者の日本語に対する自然な好奇心を満たすものになり得ないのではないか、と思っていました。

　本テキストの特徴は、①文法ではなくフレーズと機能で提示されるため自然な日本語が学べる、②場面、機能、トピックなど様々な要素からユニットを立てているため、本当に役に立つ表現を効果的に学ぶことができる、③文法編を別に作ることで、日本語とはどんな言語なのかという解説と実践練習を行き来しながら学ぶことができる、④各課に様々な形の練習が何度も出てくることで自然に表現が身につく、ということなどです。

　本テキストを使っていただく先生方にとっては、授業準備の負担が少ないように、また、比較的経験の浅い先生やボランティアの方でも使用しやすいものになるよう心がけました。テキストに沿って進めるだけでいろいろなタイプの練習が楽しめますし、特に拡張練習では、学生が自発的にクリエイティブな練習をできるようにいろいろな仕掛けがしてあります。

　作成にあたって私たちがイメージしたのは、「習ったフレーズをすぐに使ってみたくなる」「実践的かつ知的好奇心をくすぐるような大人向けの」「日本をもっと身近に感じる」テキストです。そして、その根底にあるのは、「縁あって来日した外国人の皆さんに、日本を楽しんでほしい」という想いです。
　この本を通して日本語学習者の皆さんと日本との出会いがより素敵なものになれば、心から嬉しく思います。

　2007年に作成を始めてからこの本が出版されるまでに多くの方のご協力をいただきました。
　編集担当の河野麻衣子さん、イラストレーターの平塚徳明さんは限られた時間の中でよりよい教材を作り上げるため最大限の努力をしてくださいました。教材の試用を重ね、たくさんのフィードバックを下さったいいだばし日本語学院の先生方、通常業務をより多く負担することで膨大な時間のかかる執筆活動を陰ながら支えてくださった同校スタッフの皆さん、また、私たちがこの教材を作成する原動力となった過去から現在に至るまでの全ての同校の学習者たちにも、心からの敬意と感謝を伝えたいと思います。

著者一同

Contents | 目次

【Pre-text】 Pictures | 写真資料 ··· i - iv

To Users of This Book | この本を使う方へ ··· 2
How to Use This Book | この本の使い方 ·· 6
Must-know Words and Phrases | 絶対に覚えておきたい表現 ························· 10
Explanatory Notes | 凡例 ··· 12

UNIT 1   I am John. ··· 13

Introducing yourself | 自己紹介
  Watashi wa Jon desu. / O-shigoto wa? / Ongaku ga suki desu.
  I am John. / (What is) your job? / I like music.

UNIT 2   Is there an ATM around here? ······································· 25

Asking for directions | 場所を尋ねる
  Kono hen ni, ATM arimasu ka. / Toire, doko desu ka? /
  Yūbinkyoku ni ikitai n desu ga...... .
  Is there an ATM around here? / Where is the restroom? / I'm trying to get to the post office.

UNIT 3   How much is this? ··· 37

Shopping | 買い物
  Kasa, arimasu ka. / Kore, ikura desu ka. / Kono T-shatsu, kudasai. /
  Mō chotto yasui no, arimasen ka.
  Do you have umbrellas? / How much is this? / I'll have this T-shirt. / Do you have one a little cheaper?

UNIT 4   Take out, please. ·· 51

Convenience stores and restaurants | コンビニ・レストラン
  Menyū, onegaishimasu. / Kyō no ranchi, nan desu ka. / Mochikaeri de. /
  Fukuro, kekkō desu.
  Could I have a menu? / What's the lunch of the day? / Take out, please. / No bag, thank you.

UNIT 5   Can I pay by credit card? ··· 67

Asking permission | 許可を得る
  Kādo de ii desu ka. / Kono pen, karite mo ii desu ka.
  Can I pay by credit card? / May I borrow this pen?

UNIT 6   Please wait a moment. ·· 79

Making requests | 依頼する
  Chotto matte kudasai. / Yukkuri hanashite moraemasen ka.
  Please wait a moment. / Could you speak more slowly?

UNIT 7 **Does this (train) go to Yokohama?** ···················· 91

Transportation | 交通

Kore, Yokohama ni ikimasu ka. / Shinjuku made dōyatte ikeba ii desu ka. /
Tōkyō kara Kyōto made donogurai kakarimasu ka.

Does this (train) go to Yokohama? / How do I get to Shinjuku? / How long does it take from Tokyo to Kyoto?

UNIT 8 **I'm going to an art museum.** ···················· 105

Talking about plans and activities | 予定や行動について話す

Bijutsukan ni ikimasu. / Kinō wa uchi de Nihon-go o benkyō shimashita. /
Sumō o mitai desu.

I'm going to an art museum. / I studied Japanese at home yesterday. / I want to watch sumo wrestling.

UNIT 9 **How do you like living in Japan?** ···················· 119

Talking about impressions | 感想を言う

Nihon no seikatsu wa dō desu ka. / Ryokō wa dō deshita ka.

How do you like living in Japan? / How was your trip?

UNIT 10 **What does that taste like?** ···················· 131

Eating | 食事

Sore, donna aji desu ka. / Oishisō desu ne. / Butaniku wa chotto........ .

What does that taste like? / That looks delicious. / I can't really eat pork.

UNIT 11 **It's nice weather today, isn't it?** ···················· 143

Socializing Ⅰ- Making small talk | 世間話をする

Kyō wa ii tenki desu ne. / Saikin shigoto wa dō desu ka. / Ja, mata.

It's nice weather today, isn't it? / How has your job been lately? / See you later.

UNIT 12 **Would you like to have a cup of tea?** ···················· 155

Socializing Ⅱ- Invitations | 誘う

Ocha o nomimasen ka. / Onsen ni itta koto ga arimasu ka.

Would you like to have a cup of tea? / Have you ever been to an onsen (hot spring)?

Grammar | 文法 ···················· 165

Translation of Dialogue | ダイアログ翻訳 ···················· 184

Listening Answers and CD Script | リスニング解答とスクリプト ···················· 186

【Appendix】Handy Wordbook | 別冊語彙集

How to Use This Book (To Learners)

Introduction

This book is designed to help beginner students, including those with no knowledge of the Japanese language, acquire natural-sounding, essential Japanese that can be used immediately in daily conversation. Because this book does not develop concepts of grammar as it progresses, students may begin studying from any of the 12 units at their leisure.

Particles, a grammatical device of the Japanese language, are frequently omitted as they are in daily conversation to expose students to natural sounding Japanese as much as possible. Roman letters and kana spellings to approximate the actual pronunciation of certain words are also included.

We recommend that students memorize phrases and expressions as they appear in the included dialogues so as to reproduce them later, and not analyze all elements of each sentence to study grammar.

The Grammar Appendix included at the back of the book is a complement to the main text intended to help students acquire a systematic understanding of the construction of the Japanese language. We recommend that students use the vocabulary list in the Appendix to expand exercises and practice dialogues found in the book, as well as carry around for reference of necessary words for daily conversation. The color pages in the book's pre-text include pictures of foods commonly seen in Japan, which should prove useful for daily life as well as conversation practice.

What's in a unit

Unit phrases	**Phrase 1 - 4:** Use note and example sentences to understand how phrases are used.
	Practice A: New words and practice conversation patterns. Use words from Practice A to complete phrases and communicate. Practice until you can say the words you need to know without looking at the book.
	Practice B: Short practice conversations using target phrases. Use words in Practice A to complete brief practice conversations.
General exercises	**Dialogue:** Use the target phrases in each unit to practice longer conversations. **Listening:** Practice listening exercises with Japanese spoken at a natural speed. **Do you remember?:** Use the right word or sentence as indicated by an illustration to see if you have learned target phrases. **Role playing:** Perform role play exercises using the expressions learned in that unit. **Phrases for This Unit:** Review the phrases learned in a unit in addition to other crucial expressions.
Other pages	**Material:** A page of items to help effectively perform practice conversations. **One More Step:** Practice for students wanting to challenge themselves to more difficult expressions. **Remember and Use!:** A page to help students memorize basic Japanese words, including numbers, verbs, and adjectives, for later use. **Good to Know:** Helpful introductions to services and Japanese words and phrases that make life in Japan a breeze.

この本の使い方（先生方へ）

はじめに

　本テキストは、日本語の知識が全くない人から初級前半程度の文法を習得している学習者が、日常生活で必要なすぐに使える自然な日本語を習得できるように作られた教材です。

　本テキストは文法積み上げ式のテキストではありませんので、全部で12あるユニットのうちのどのユニットからでも学習を始めることができます。学習者の希望やレベルに合わせて使用する課をピックアップしたり、ユニットの順番を変えて使用しても問題ありません。

　UNIT 1から12まで順に学習を進めていくときには、既習ユニットの文型を取り入れながら学習を拡張していけるような練習も含まれており、効果的な学習をすることができます。

　なるべく自然な日本語に触れてもらえるように、日常的に使われている助詞の省略などはそのまま表記しました。またローマ字表記も、音声と近い表記を採用しました。

　フレーズや談話に出てくる表現については、ひとつずつ分解して文法的な説明を加えるのではなく、そのままフレーズとして覚えることを想定しています。そのため、教師は教えるというよりも、そのフレーズの使用場面を想定した会話練習を一緒にしたり、フレーズや語彙を覚えやすいようにサポートする役割が期待されます。

　動詞や形容詞の活用についても、そのユニット内の会話練習で必要な形だけを練習し、活用形の作り方は教えません。そのような文法的な解説は、文法編にまとめて掲載してあります。ただし、基本練習をしたい人向けに、UNIT 8とUNIT 9のあとのRemember and Use! で、動詞と形容詞の時制・肯定形・否定形の活用練習ができるようになっています。

　文法編は、学習者が日本語の仕組みを体系的に理解できるような読み物としてあり、本文と関連しています。別冊語彙集は、Practice Aの代入練習や談話練習などで学習者がより幅広い語彙から練習をできるように、また、持ち運び可能な単語集としても利用できるよう別冊として付属させました。また、巻頭のカラー料理写真もぜひ練習に活用してください。

　本テキストをメイン教材として利用する場合には、授業内でPractice Aの語彙の定着をはかりながら進めていくのが効果的です。また、サブテキストとして使用する場合には、提出されている語彙だけでなく、学習者の使いたい語彙や場面を取り上げて練習を膨らませていくのがよいでしょう。

1ユニットの構成と授業の流れ

① 学習目標の確認・動機づけ

　ユニット扉には、学習するフレーズの使用場面と学習目標（ゴール）が書いてあります。

　まずはここを読んで、これから学習するフレーズがどんな場面で使われるものなのか、また、このユニットを学習することで何ができるようになるのか、という学習目標の確認をし、学習の動機づけを行いましょう。

② フレーズ導入（各ユニットに2〜4のフレーズがあります。）

NOTEとEX.で、フレーズの機能と意味の確認をします。

クラスではホワイトボードやなどを使って本日の学習内容としてのフレーズ提示を行うと流れをうまく作ることができます。

③ フレーズ練習

Practice Aのパターン練習をします。

語彙の確認：教師が指導する場合にはどこまでを覚えさせる語彙とするのかしっかり目標を決めて語彙導入、練習を行うのが効果的です。特に教室ではできるだけカードなどで繰り返し語彙の提示を行って定着を図ってください。

代入練習：フレーズにPractice Aの語彙を代入した文を言わせます。なるべく文字を追わずにフレーズを言わせるようにしましょう。学習者にあったスピードで、可能な場合は自然なスピードに近づけていってみましょう。

④ 談話練習

Practice Bでフレーズを使った談話練習をします。

談話の意味確認：読み合わせ後、下のMEMOや英訳でわからない語彙を確認し、談話の場面をしっかりと理解させてください。問題文の指示にしたがって、＜　＞にPratice Aの語彙などを入れ替えながら、談話練習をしてください。ここでも、なるべく文字を見ずに談話ができるよう繰り返し練習を行ってください。

本テキストでは、UNIT 1〜UNIT 7をサバイバルパート、UNIT 8〜UNIT 12をコミュニケーションパートと位置づけています。サバイバルパートでは日本人と外国人役がはっきりしている談話が多いので、教師と行う際には教師が店員や駅員などの日本人役を担当するようにしましょう。

⑤ 総合談話練習

Dialogueでユニット内の複数のフレーズを使った談話練習をします。

ユニット内で出てきた複数のフレーズをひとつの場面の中で使ってみる総合的な談話練習です。本文内に英訳がないので、読み合わせをして学習者の理解度を確認してから練習に入ってください。談話の理解や入れ替えを助けるために、右ページにMaterialがつけられていることもあります。これもできるだけ文字を追わずに談話ができるよう繰り返し練習を行ってください。また、可能な場合は学習者のオリジナルパターンを作ってみるよう促してみてください。

⑥ リスニング練習

Listeningで、ユニットで学習したフレーズを使った会話の聞き取り練習をします。

各ユニットに4問出題されます。自然に近いスピードで話されているので、全てを聞き取るのではなく必要な情報のスキャンする能力を高めることを目指しています。

⑦ ロールプレイ練習

　Role playing で、学習したフレーズを使って自分で会話を組み立てる練習をします。

　必ず決まった答えがあるわけではないので、ロールカードを見て、ここまでの学習内容を応用し、自分なりの会話を組み立てるように促しましょう。既にいくつかのユニットを学習済みであれば、既習のフレーズや語彙も会話に盛り込めるように教師が学習者をリードできると、より効果的です。

⑧ 場面練習

　Do you remember? では、日常場面で起こりがちな場面のイラストを見て、学習したフレーズがぱっと出てくるかを確認する練習をします。

　フレーズの確認だけでなく、そこから会話を発展させたり、その場面で考えられる他の会話を考えるなど、応用練習の素材としても活用してください。

⑨ フレーズ復習・到達度チェック

　Phrases for This Unit では、ユニットに出てきたターゲットフレーズと、談話練習で出てきた便利な表現をまとめてあるので、1ユニットの内容を簡単に振り返ることができます。

　また、ユニットの最後の項目では、ユニット扉で設定した学習目標が達成できたかどうかをチェックすることができます。

⑩ その他

　Remember and Use! : 最低限覚えておきたい動詞や形容詞、数字を定着させるための練習ページです。場面会話だけでなく文章作成の力もつけたい人にお勧めです。また、このコーナーをユニット学習に入る前に学習しておくのも効果的です。

　One More Step: メインの学習項目に加えて、更に高度な語彙や表現に挑戦できるよう作られたページです。

　Good to Know : 日本の生活の中で知っておくと便利なサービス、日本語の仕組みや運用に関する情報を紹介するコーナーです。

参考カリキュラム例

・30時間コース

　メインユニット練習 … 約24時間：UNIT 1 〜 12（1ユニット2時間 x 12ユニット）

　定着・応用練習 ……… 約6時間：Remember & Use!、One More Step

・20時間コース

　メインユニット練習 … 約14時間：UNIT 1 〜 7（1ユニット2時間 x 7ユニット）

　定着・応用練習 ……… 約6時間：絶対に覚えておきたい表現、Remember & Use!

Must-know Words and Phrases | 絶対に覚えておきたい表現

● Survival Phrases

1. すみません。*
   Sumimasen. *

   Sorry. / Excuse me. / Thank you.

   *An all-purpose phrase that can be used when calling out to a person, apologizing, or thanking someone.

2. a) はい。　b) いいえ。
   a) Hai.　b) Iie.

   a) Yes.　b) No.

3. a) そうです。　b) ちがいます。
   a) Sō desu.　b) Chigaimasu.

   a) That' right.　b) That's wrong. / No.

4. 英語は話せますか。
   えいご　はな
   Eigo wa hanasemasu ka.

   Do you speak English?

5. 英語が話せる人はいますか。
   えいご　はな　ひと
   Eigo ga hanaseru hito wa imasu ka.

   Is there anyone (here) who speaks English?

6. Q: わかりますか。
   Q: Wakarimasu ka.

   Q: Do you understand?

   A: a) わかります。　b) わかりません。
   A: a) Wakarimasu.　b) Wakarimasen.

   A: a) I understand.　b) I don't understand.

7. Q: わかりましたか。
   Q: Wakarimashita ka.

   Q: Did you get that? / Did that make sense?

   A: a) わかりました。　b) わかりません。
   A: a) Wakarimashita.　b) Wakarimasen.

   A: a) I got it.　b) I don't get it.

8. 日本語はわかりません。
   に ほん ご
   Nihon-go wa wakarimasen.

   I don't understand Japanese.

9. Q: 大丈夫ですか。
   だいじょう ぶ
   Q: Daijōbu desu ka.

   Q: Are you alright?

   A: 大丈夫です。
   だいじょう ぶ
   A: Daijōbu desu.

   A: I'm alright.

10. Q: いいですか。
    Q: Ii desu ka.

    Q: Can I ...? / Is it okay?

    A: a) どうぞ。　b) すみません、ちょっと……。
    A: a) Dōzo.　b) Sumimasen, chotto….

    A: a) Please./Okay./Go ahead.　b) Sorry, but... .

11. もう一度いいですか。
    いちど
    Mō ichido ii desu ka.

    Would you say that one more time?

● Greetings

1. おはよう（ございます）。
   Ohayō (gozaimasu).

   Good morning.

2. こんにちは。
   Konnichiwa.

   Hello. / Good afternoon.

3. こんばんは。
   Kombanwa.

   Good evening.

4. ありがとう（ございます）。
   Arigatō (gozaimasu).

   Thank you (very much).

5. いただきます。
   Itadakimasu.

   I humbly receive this food.
   [said before a meal]

6. ごちそうさま（でした）。
   Gochisōsama (deshita).

   Thank you.
   [a set phrase said at the end of a meal]

● Helpful Words and Phrases

1. （お）元気ですか。*
   (O)genki desu ka. *

   How are you?
   *Typically not asked to people seen on a daily basis.

2. 元気です。
   Genki desu.

   I'm fine.

3. がんばって（ください）。
   Gambatte (kudasai).

   Do your best. / Good luck. / Break a leg.

4. どうぞ。
   Dōzo.

   Go ahead. / Please.

5. どうも。
   Dōmo.

   Thanks. [casual]

6. すごい
   sugoi

   Awesome/amazing/great/a lot

7. 本当
   hontō

   Really/true

8. もちろん
   mochiron

   Of course

● Numbers

1	2	3	4	5	6	7	8	9	10
いち	に	さん	よん / し	ご	ろく	なな / しち	はち	きゅう / く	じゅう
ichi	ni	san	yon / shi	go	roku	nana / shichi	hachi	kyū / ku	jū

Explanatory Notes | 凡例

A note about *kana* / *kanji* and the Romanization

Because this book is designed to help learners acquire conversational skills regardless of their ability to read Japanese, text is displayed in both a mixture of *kana* and *kanji* as well as Roman letters. However, some areas of the book only feature Roman letters due to space constraints.

Kanji are printed wherever they would normally be used in written Japanese, along with their readings in *hiragana*.

This book mainly incorporates the Hepburn system of Romanization.

Long vowels are indicated with a horizontal line (eg. Tōkyō = Tookyoo).

However, the long [i] found at the end i-adjectives, such as in "tanoshii" are spelled out to more easily demonstrate conjugations. Long [e] sounds are written as "ee" or "ei" depending on the original spelling of the word in question, although many times words with an [ei] sound are pronounced more like [ee].

Compound words include hyphens to indicate boundaries between individual words to aid pronunciation, such as "100-en" and "hon-ya".

Characters in this book

Jon

ジョン／John
American, Engineer

Karen

カレン／Karen
British, John's wife/
English teacher

Kumāru

クマール／Kumar
Indian, John's co-worker/
Engineer

Tanaka

田中／Tanaka
た なか
Japanese, John's co-worker in
the general affairs division

Satō

佐藤／Sato
さ とう
Japanese, John and Karen's
friend/Student

Suzuki

鈴木／Suzuki
すず き
Japanese, John and Karen's
friend/Housewife

I am John.

私はジョンです。
<ruby>私<rt>わたし</rt></ruby>

Watashi wa Jon desu.

Introducing yourself

自己紹介

GOALS FOR UNIT 1

- Provide a simple self-introduction

- Ask a person you just met for their name and occupation

- Have a conversation about hobbies and interests

Phrase 1 — Introducing oneself.

私 はジョンです。
わたし

Watashi **wa** Jon **desu.**　　　　　　　　**I am** John.

Track 1

NOTE **"A wa B desu"** means **"A = B"**. **"wa"** marks the topic/subject of the sentence, while **"desu"** means something similar to **"to be"** in English, and comes after a noun or adjective in polite sentences. Japanese speakers often omit the topic, or **"____wa"** portion of a sentence, when the identity of the topic is obvious from context.

Ex.

ジョン ：私はジョンです。
　　　　 わたし

　　　　（私は）アメリカ人です。どうぞよろしく。
　　　　　わたし　　　　　 じん

Jon　　　: Watashi **wa** Jon **desu.**
　　　　　(Watashi wa) Amerika-jin **desu.** Dōzo yoroshiku.

John　　: I am John.
　　　　　(I'm) American.
　　　　　It's nice to meet you.

Practice A

私は_____です。
わたし

Let's use the following words with the phrase **"Watashi wa ____desu."**

ジョン	アメリカ人 じん	エンジニア
Jon	Amerika-jin*1	enjinia
John	American	engineer
→ "Your name"	→ *See Appendix, Countries*	→ *See Appendix, Jobs*

Jobs	学生 がく せい	先生／教師 せん せい　きょう し	会社員 かい しゃ いん	主婦 しゅ ふ
	gakusei	sensei / kyōshi*2	kaishain	shufu
	student	teacher	company worker	housewife

Countries	日本 に ほん	インド	イギリス	オーストラリア
	Nihon	Indo	Igirisu	Ōsutoraria
	Japan	India	United Kingdom	Australia

＊1 "[country]+ jin" = people / person from that country / area.

＊2 Use "kyōshi" for yourself and the respectful "sensei" for another person.

14

B-1 Provide a self-introduction with the words found in Practice A.

ジョン　：はじめまして。私<small>わたし</small>は〈ジョン〉です。

〈エンジニア〉です。〈アメリカ〉人<small>じん</small>です。どうぞよろしく。

クマール：〈クマール〉です。〈インド〉から来<small>き</small>ました。

こちらこそ、どうぞよろしく。

Jon 　　 : Hajimemashite. Watashi wa <Jon> desu.

　　　　 <Enjinia> desu. <Amerika>-jin desu.

　　　　 Dōzo yoroshiku.

Kumāru 　: <Kumāru> desu. <Indo> kara kimashita.

　　　　 Kochira koso, dōzo yoroshiku.

> Jon 　　 : How do you do. I'm John.
> 　　　　　 I'm an engineer. I'm American.
> 　　　　　 It's nice to meet you.
> Kumar 　: I'm Kumar. I'm from India.
> 　　　　　 The pleasure is mine.

 B-2 Ask for the listener's job and nationality using the words in Practice A.

佐藤　　：ジョンさんは〈学生<small>がくせい</small>〉ですか。

ジョン　：いいえ、〈学生<small>がくせい</small>〉じゃありません。* 〈エンジニア〉です。

Satō 　 : Jon-san wa <gakusei> desu ka.

Jon 　　 : Iie, <gakusei> ja arimasen.*

　　　　 <Enjinia> desu.

> Sato 　 : Are you a <student>, John-san?
> John 　 : No, I'm not a < student >.
> 　　　　　 I'm an < engineer >.

* To answer affirmatively, say "Hai, gakusei desu."

MEMO

はじめまして。／Hajimemashite.／How do you do?

どうぞよろしく。／Dōzo yoroshiku.／It's nice to meet you.

〜から来<small>き</small>ました。／… kara kimashita.／(I'm) from … .

こちらこそ／kochira koso／an emphatic way to say "I'm the one" that can be translated as "me too"

〜か。／… ka.／Add "ka" to the end of a declarative sentence to make it question. Ex. Jon-san desu ka? = Are you John?

はい／いいえ／hai / iie／yes / no

(Aは)Bじゃありません。／(A wa) B ja arimasen.／A is not B.

Phrase 2 — Ask the listener for information about him/herself.

お仕事は？
しごと

O-shigoto **wa?**　　　　　　　　**(What is)** your job?

Track
2

> **NOTE** "____**wa?**" is an abbreviated version of a question. Japanese speakers often omit the question words of a sentence and only state the topic when it is obvious they are asking a question from context. Rising intonation signifies that the "____**wa?**" statement is an abbreviated question. Ex. **O-shigoto wa?** (↗)

Ex.

①田中：<u>お仕事</u>**は**（なんですか）？　　ジョン：エンジニアです。
　たなか　　しごと

②田中：<u>お住まい</u>**は**（どこですか）？　　ジョン：千葉です。
　たなか　　す　　　　　　　　　　　　　　　　　　　　ちば

①Tanaka　：<u>O-shigoto</u> **wa (nan desu ka)** ?
　Jon　　　：Enjinia desu.

②Tanaka　：<u>O-sumai</u> **wa (doko desu ka)** ?
　Jon　　　：Chiba desu.

①Tanaka　：(What is) your job?
　John　　 ：(I'm) an engineer.

②Tanaka　：(Where do) you live?
　John　　 ：(I live) in Chiba.

A　____は？
Use the following words with the phrase "____ **wa?**"

（お*)仕事 しごと (O*)shigoto job → **See Appendix, Jobs**	（お）国 くに (O)kuni country → **See Appendix, Countries**	（ご*)出身 しゅっしん (Go*)shusshin birth place/hometown
（お）名前 なまえ (O)namae name	（お）住まい／（お）うち す (O)sumai / (O)uchi home / place of residence	（お）勤め／会社 つと　　かいしゃ (O)tsutome / kaisha company

＊ Attaching the prefix お **(o)** or ご **(go)** to a noun makes that noun polite. Use these prefixes when talking about another person, and never for yourself.　→ See p.183, Grammar

16

Practice B-1 Place your own name and information in <   > to complete the following sentences.

鈴木
すずき　：〈ジョン〉さん、お国は？
　　　　　　　　　　　くに

ジョン　：〈アメリカ〉です。

鈴木
すずき　：お住まいは？
　　　　す

ジョン　：〈千葉〉です。〈鈴木〉さんは？
　　　　　ち ば　　　　すず き

鈴木
すずき　：私も〈千葉〉です。／私は〈東京〉です。
　　　わたし　ち ば　　　　　　とうきょう

ジョン　：お仕事は？
　　　　し ごと

鈴木
すずき　：〈主婦〉です。
　　　　しゅ ふ

Suzuki : Jon-san, o-kuni wa?	Suzuki : Where are you from, John-san?
Jon : < Amerika > desu.	John : I'm from the United States.
Suzuki : O-sumai wa?	Suzuki : Where do you live?
Jon : <Chiba > desu. < Suzuki >-san wa?	John : I live in Chiba. How about you, Suzuki-san?
Suzuki : Watashi mo <Chiba > desu. /	Suzuki : I live in Chiba, too. /
Watashi wa < Tōkyō> desu.	I live in Tokyo.
Jon : O-shigoto wa?	John : What is your job.
Suzuki : < Shufu > desu.	Suzuki : I'm a housewife.

Practice B-2 Make your own conversation using the words in practice A.

MEMO

私も〜です。／Watashi mo … desu.／I'm also ….
わたし

Phrase 3 — Talk about your interests.

音楽が好きです。
おんがく　す

Ongaku **ga suki desu.**　　　　　　　**I like** music.

Track 3

NOTE　**"[Noun] ga suki desu"** means **"I like [noun]."** → See p.169, Grammar
In sentences like the examples below, the **"watashi wa____"** portion of the sentence
that denotes the subject is often omitted in spoken conversation.

Ex.

ジョン　：（私は）音楽が好きです。
　　　　　わたし　　おんがく　す
　　　　　でも、カラオケは好きじゃありません。
　　　　　　　　　　　　　　す

Jon　　: (Watashi wa) ongaku **ga suki desu.**
　　　　Demo, karaoke wa suki ja arimasen.

John　　: I like music.
　　　　　　　But, I don't like karaoke.

Practice A

____が好きです。
　　す
Use the following words with the phrase "_____ **ga suki desu.**"

音楽 おん がく ongaku music	映画 えい が eiga movie	カラオケ karaoke karaoke
アウトドア autodoa the outdoors	旅行 りょ こう ryokō travel → *See Appendix, Hobbies*	サッカー sakkā soccer/football → *See Appendix, Sports*
（お）すし (O)sushi sushi → *See Appendix, Food*	ビール bīru beer → *See Appendix, Drinks*	イタリア料理 りょう り Itaria ryōri Italian food → *See Appendix, Countries*

18

B Use words from practice A in < > to practice having a conversation.

1 ···

鈴木
すずき :私は〈ビール〉が好きです。カレンさんは？
　　　　わたし　　　　　　す

カレン :私も好きです。／私はあまり好きじゃありません。
　　　　わたし　す　　　　わたし　　　す

Suzuki : Watashi wa < bīru > ga suki desu.

　　　　Karen-san wa?

Karen　: Watashi mo suki desu.

　　　　/ Watashi wa amari suki ja arimasen.

> Suzuki　:I like beer. How about you, Karen-san?
> Karen　　:I like beer, too. / I don't really like beer.

2 ···

田中
たなか :〈カラオケ〉は*好きですか。
　　　　　　　　　　す

ジョン :はい、好きです。
　　　　　　す

　　　　／いいえ、〈カラオケ〉はあまり……。でも〈音楽〉は好きです。
　　　　　　　　　　　　　　　　　　　　　　　おんがく　す

田中
たなか :そうですか。

Tanaka : Karaoke wa suki desu ka.

Jon　　: Hai, suki desu.

　　　　/ Iie, karaoke wa amari... .

　　　　Demo, ongaku wa suki desu.

Tanaka : Sō desu ka.

> Tanaka : Do you like karaoke?
> John　 : Yes, I do.
> 　　　　　/ No, not really. But, I like music.
> Tanaka : I see.

MEMO

あまり／amari／not very much, not really

でも／demo／but

そうですか。／Sō desu ka.／I see.

*は(wa) can be used to denote a topic or subject, it can also be used to imply a comparison or contrast. Because of this nuance, は(wa) often appears instead of が(ga) in statements that contain a nuance of comparison, such as negative or interrogative sentences, like in the example sentence above.

Dialogue

Practice having a conversation by replacing the words in (1)－(3) with the words below. Put your own name and information in < >.

ジョン ：はじめまして。〈ジョン〉です。
　　　　どうぞよろしく。

田中 ：はじめまして。〈田中〉です。
　　　　こちらこそ、どうぞよろしく
　　　　お願いします。
　　　　ジョンさん、(1)お国は？

ジョン ：〈アメリカ〉です。

田中 ：そうですか。(2)お住まいは？

ジョン ：〈千葉〉です。〈田中さん〉は？

田中 ：私は〈中野〉です。
　　　　ジョンさん、(3)日本料理は好き
　　　　ですか。

ジョン ：はい、〈天ぷら〉が好きです。
　　　　／いいえ、あまり……。

田中 ：そうですか。

Jon : Hajimemashite. < Jon > desu.
　　　Dōzo yoroshiku.

Tanaka : Hajimemashite. < Tanaka > desu.
　　　Kochira koso, dōzo yoroshiku
　　　onegaishimasu.
　　　Jon-san, (1) o-kuni wa?

Jon : < Amerika > desu.

Tanaka : Sō desu ka. (2) O-sumai wa?

Jon : < Chiba > desu. < Tanaka >-san wa?

Tanaka : Watashi wa < Nakano > desu.
　　　Jon-san, (3) Nihon-ryōri wa suki desu
　　　ka.

Jon : Hai, < tempura > ga suki desu.
　　　/ Iie, amari.......

Tanaka : Sō desu ka.

---

①
(1) ご出身　　　　go-shusshin
(2) お仕事　　　　o-shigoto
(3) スポーツ　　　supōtsu

②
(1) お国　　　　　o-kuni
(2) お勤め　　　　o-tsutome
(3) お酒　　　　　o-sake

Listening

Two people who just met are having a conversation. Listen to what they say and select the correct answer.

Q1

1. The man is English.
2. The man is Australian.
3. The man is Indian.

Q2

1. The woman asked the man for his name and hometown.
2. The woman asked the man where he works and lives.
3. The woman asked the man about his hometown and job.

Q3

1. The woman doesn't like karaoke.
2. The man likes karaoke.
3. The man doesn't like karaoke.

Q4

1. The woman likes wine.
2. The woman doesn't like alcohol.
3. The man likes beer.

Role playing

Role play using the cards below.

At a party

A: You meet B-san, a Japanese person, for the first time at a friend's party. Say hello to B-san and introduce yourself. (Please use your own answers.)

B: You are a Japanese person. Ask where A-san is from, where he/she works and lives in Japan, what he/she likes, and what his/her interests are.

Do you remember?

Use the phrases you have learned in this unit in situations ①–③ below.

①

- Name
- Job
- Nationality

I'm ….

②

Where are you from?

③

Do you like …?

Phrases for This Unit

Unit Phrases

● 私はジョンです。 わたし	Watashi wa Jon desu.	I am John.
● お仕事は？ し ごと	O-shigoto wa?	(What is) your job?
● 音楽が好きです。 おんがく す	Ongaku ga suki desu.	I like music.

Useful expressions

● ～から来ました。 き	... kara kimashita.	I'm from ....
● どうぞよろしく	Dōzo yoroshiku.	It's nice to meet you.

Check!

Now I can...

☐ Provide a simple self-introduction

☐ Ask a person I just met for their name and occupation

☐ Have a conversation about hobbies and interests

One More Step

● Talking about family

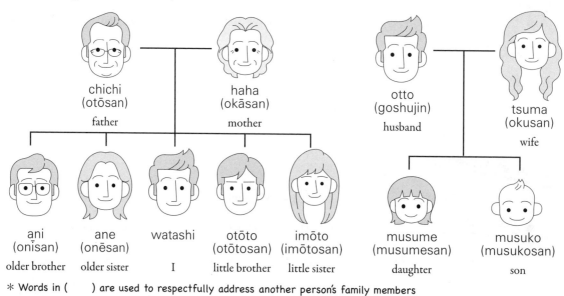

chichi
(otōsan)
father

haha
(okāsan)
mother

otto
(goshujin)
husband

tsuma
(okusan)
wife

ani
(onīsan)
older brother

ane
(onēsan)
older sister

watashi
I

otōto
(otōtosan)
little brother

imōto
(imōtosan)
little sister

musume
(musumesan)
daughter

musuko
(musukosan)
son

* Words in (   ) are used to respectfully address another person's family members

Let's practice

(1) Use the examples below to describe where your family members are from (a), what they do (b), and where they live (c).

    a. Watashi no*1 tsuma wa Igirisu-jin desu.

    b. Watashi no haha wa kyōshi desu.

    c. Watashi no musuko wa Ōsutoraria ni sunde imasu.*2

(2) Fill in the blanks below to have a conversation about someone's siblings and children.

    Q. Go-kyōdai*3 / okosan*4 ga imasu ka.*5

    A. a. Hai, _____ to*6 _____ ga imasu.

       b. Hai, _____ ga [number] imasu.

       c. Iie, imasen.

Counting people

one person	hitori
two people	futari
three people	san-nin
four people	yo-nin

Say the number word + **nin** when counting three or more people

*1 watashi no = my   *2 …wa [place] ni sunde imasu = … live in [place]   *3 go-kyōdai = (Your) brothers and sisters ("kyōdai" refers to one's own siblings)   *4 okosan = (Your) children ("kodomo" refers to one's own children)   *5 … ga imasu ka. = Do you have … ? (for animate objects)
→ *See p.170, Grammar* *6 A to B = A and B

Is there an ATM around here?

このへんに、ATMありますか。

Kono hen ni , ATM arimasu ka.

Asking for directions

場所を尋ねる

GOALS FOR UNIT 2

- Ask if a store or place you want to go to is in the nearby area

- Ask for the location of a store or place you want to go to

- Ask and understand simple directions

Phrase 1

Ask if a store or place you want to go to is in the nearby area.

このへんに、ATMありますか。

Kono hen ni, ATM arimasu ka.   Is there an ATM around here?

Track
9

<u>NOTE</u> "___ (wa) arimasu ka?" = "Is there ___?", "Kono hen ni" means "around here."
"Arimasu" is used only for inanimate objects. → *See p.170, Grammar*

Ex.

ジョン ：すみません。**このへんに、**<u>ATM</u>（は）**ありますか。**

女の人 ：ええ、あそこにありますよ。
おんな ひと

Jon   : Sumimasen. **Kono hen ni,**
              <u>ATM</u> **(wa) arimasu ka.**

Onna no hito : Ee, asoko ni arimasu yo.

John   : Excuse me. Is there an ATM
              around here?
Woman : Yes, over there.

Practice
A

このへんに、_____、ありますか。
Use the following words with the phrase **"Kono hen ni, ___ arimasu ka."**

ATM	地下鉄の駅	バス停
ATM	ちかてつ　えき	てい
ATM	chikatetsu no eki	basu-tei
	subway station	bus stop

交番	駐車場	コンビニ
こう ばん	ちゅうしゃ じょう	
kōban	chūshajō	kombini
police box	parking lot	convenience store
		→ *See Appendix, Shops*

インターネットカフェ	スーパー	100円ショップ	薬屋
		えん	くすり や
intānetto kafe	sūpā	hyaku-en shoppu	kusuri-ya
internet café	super market	100-yen store	drugstore

Practice B Put the words from Practice A into <   > to complete the exercise.

1

-On a street-

ジョン ：すみません。このへんに、〈コンビニ〉ありますか。

女の人 ：ええ、あそこにありますよ。
おんな ひと

ジョン ：ありがとうございます。

女の人 ：どういたしまして。
おんな ひと

Jon	: Sumimasen. Kono hen ni < kombini > arimasu ka.
Onna no hito	: Ee, asoko ni arimasu yo.
Jon	: Arigatō gozaimasu.
Onna no hito	: Dō itashimashite.

> John : Excuse me, is there a convenience store around here?
> Woman : Yes, it's over there.
> John : Thank you.
> Woman : You're welcome.

2

-On a street-

ジョン ：すみません。このへんに、〈薬屋〉ありますか。
くすり や

男の人 ：さあ、ちょっとわかりません。
おとこ ひと

ジョン ：じゃ、いいです。ありがとうございます。

Jon	: Sumimasen. Kono hen ni <kusuri-ya> arimasu ka.
Otoko no hito	: Sā, chotto wakarimasen.
Jon	: Ja, ii desu. Arigatō gozaimasu.

> John : Excuse me, is there a drug store around here?
> Man : Hmm, I'm not sure [if there is].
> John : That's alright. Thank you.

MEMO

ええ／ee／yes

あそこにありますよ。／Asoko ni arimasu yo.／It's over there. *The particle "yo" is used to emphasize new information to a person.

どういたしまして。／Dō itashimashite.／You're welcome.

さあ／sā／I don't know. [said to indicate a lack of sureness]

ちょっとわかりません。／Chotto wakarimasen.／I'm not sure.

じゃ、いいです。／Ja, ii desu.／That's alright.

Phrase 2　　Ask where something is.

トイレ、どこですか。

Toire, **doko desu ka.**

Where is the restroom?

Track 10

> **NOTE** "Doko" means "where.", " _____(wa) doko desu ka." is used to ask for the location of something.

Ex.

ジョン ：すみません。<u>トイレ</u>（は）どこですか。

店員 ：こちらです。
てんいん

Jon 　　: Sumimasen. <u>Toire</u> **(wa) doko desu ka.**
Ten'in : Kochira desu.

> John 　: Excuse me. Where is the restroom?
> Clerk 　: This way.

A-1 _____、どこですか。
Use the following words with the phrase "_____ , doko desu ka."

トイレ	レジ	エレベーター
toire	reji	erebētā
restroom	cash register	elevator
コインロッカー	入り口 い　　ぐち	本屋 ほん　や
koin rokkā	iriguchi	hon-ya
coin locker	entrance	bookstore → **See Appendix, Shops**

A-2 _____です。
Answer the questions from above using the following words with the phrase "_____ desu."

ここ／こちら*	そこ／そちら*	あそこ／あちら*
koko / kochira*	soko / sochira*	asoko / achira*
here / this way	there / that way	over there / that way

28

* Kochira, sochira, and achira are polite versions of these expressions.

1階 いっ かい ikkai first floor	2階 に かい ni-kai second floor	3階 さん かい san-kai third floor	4階 よん かい yon-kai fourth floor

＊ Please see **Counters** on p.178 of **Grammar** for counting floors higher than 4.

 B-1 Have a practice conversation using the words from practice A-1 and A-2 in <   >

ジョン　：すみません、^{A-1}〈トイレ〉、どこですか。

店員　　：^{A-2}〈あちら〉です。
てんいん

ジョン　：ありがとうございます。

Jon　　　: Sumimasen, ^{A-1}< toire >, doko desu ka.

Ten'in　: ^{A-2}< Achira > desu.

Jon　　　: Arigatō gozaimasu.

> John　: Excuse me, where is the restroom?
> Clerk　: It's over that way.
> John　: Thank you.

 B-2 Ask what floor the following shops are on with the conversation pattern below.

1. Bookstore　　2. 100-yen store　　3. Restaurants

-At the reception desk-

ジョン　：すみません、〈　　〉は何階ですか。
　　　　　　　　　　　　　　なんかい

受付　　：〈　　〉でございます。
うけつけ

ジョン　：え？もう一度いいですか。
　　　　　　　　　　いち ど

受付　　：〈　　〉です。
うけつけ

Jon　　　　　: Sumimasen, < > wa nan-kai desu ka.

Uketsuke　: < > kai de gozaimasu.

Jon　　　　　: E? Mō ichido ii desu ka.

Uketsuke　: < > desu.

4F	Restaurants
3F	Bookstore
2F	100-yen store
1F	Reception / Front desk

> John　: Excuse me, what floor is the < > on?
> Clerk　: It's on the < >.
> John　: Pardon? Would you say that one more time?
> Clerk　: It's < >.

MEMO

もう一度いいですか。／Mō ichido ii desu ka.／Would you say that one more time?
　いち ど

〜は何階ですか。／... wa nan-kai desu ka.／What floor is the ... on?
　　なん かい

Phrase 3 — Gather information about a place you are trying to go.

郵便局に行きたいんですが……。
ゆうびんきょく　い

Track
11

Yūbinkyoku ni **ikitai n desu ga……** .   **I'm trying to get to** the post office.

> NOTE "__ ni ikitai" means " I would like to go to __" or "I am trying to get to __".
> "__ n desu ga" frequently precedes a sentence requesting information, but because this nuance is so obvious from context, the rest of the sentence following "__ n desu ga" is often left out.

Ex.

ジョン　：すみません。郵便局に行きたいんですが……。
　　　　　　　　　　　ゆうびんきょく　い

警察官　：あの公園の左ですよ。
けいさつかん　　こうえん　ひだり

Jon : Sumimasen. Yūbinkyoku ni ikitai n desu ga...... .	John : Excuse me, I'm trying to get to the post office, but....
Keisatsu-kan : Ano kōen no hidari desu yo.	Policeman : It's to the left of that park.

Practice
A-1

_____に行きたいんですが……。
　　　　い
Use the following words with the phrase " _____ ni ikitai n desu ga...... ."

郵便局
ゆう びん きょく
yūbinkyoku
post office

映画館
えい が かん
eigakan
movie theater

銀行
ぎん こう
ginkō
bank

動物園
どう ぶつ えん
dōbutsu-en
zoo

公園
こう えん
kōen
park

病院
びょういん
byōin
hospital

美術館
び じゅつ かん
bijutsukan
art museum

Practice
A-2

_____ですよ。
Answer the questions from above using the following words with the phrase " _____ desu yo."

ここまっすぐ
koko massugu
straight up / down here

あっち

acchi
over that way

むこう

mukō
over there

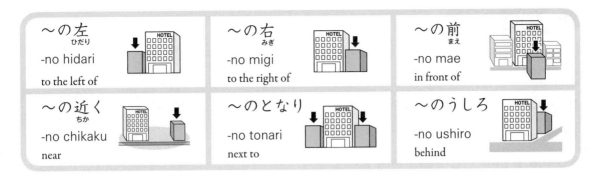

~の左 ひだり -no hidari to the left of	~の右 みぎ -no migi to the right of	~の前 まえ -no mae in front of
~の近く ちか -no chikaku near	~のとなり -no tonari next to	~のうしろ -no ushiro behind

B Practice　Look at the map on p. 33 and ask for items 1-4 with the conversation template below.

Ex. ふじ病院　Fuji byōin
びょういん

1. 本屋　hon-ya　2. 映画館　eigakan　3. さくらホテル　Sakura hoteru　4. 郵便局　yūbinkyoku
ほん や　　　　　えい が かん　　　　　　　　　　　　　　　　　　　　　　　　ゆうびん きょく

ジョン　：すみません、〈ふじ病院〉に行きたいんですが……。
　　　　　　　　　　　　びょういん

警察官　：〈ここまっすぐ〉ですよ。／〈美術館の前〉ですよ。
けいさつかん　　　　　　　　　　　　　　び じゅつかん　まえ

ジョン　：近いですか。
　　　　　ちか

警察官　：はい、近いですよ。／いいえ、ちょっと遠いですよ。
けいさつかん　　　　ちか　　　　　　　　　　　　　　　とお

Jon	: Sumimasen, \<Fuji byōin \>　ni ikitai n desu ga... .	John	: Excuse me, I'm trying to get to Fuji Hospital.
Keisatsu-kan	: \<Koko massugu\> desu yo.　/ \<Bijutsukan no mae\> desu yo.	Policeman	: It's straight down here. / It's in front of the museum.
Jon	: Chikai desu ka.	John	: Is it near here?
Keisatsu-kan	: Hai, chikai desu yo.　/ Iie, chotto tōi desu yo.	Policeman	: Yes. / No, it's a little far.

MEMO

近いですか。／Chikai desu ka.／Is it near here?
ちか

ちょっと遠いですよ。／Chotto tōi desu yo.／It's a little far.
　　　とお

Dialogue

Track 12

Look at the picture on the right page and have a practice conversation replacing the words in (1) - (4).

-In front of a station-

クマール	：すみません。	Kumāru	: Sumimasen.
女の人	：はい。	Onna no hito	: Hai.
クマール	：(1)<u>さくら公園</u>に行きたいんですが……。	Kumāru	: (1) <u>Sakura kōen</u> ni ikitai n desu ga...... .
女の人	：えっと……、ここまっすぐですよ。	Onna no hito	: Etto......, koko massugu desu yo.
クマール	：そうですか。あ、それから、このへんに、(2)<u>ATM</u>ありますか。	Kumāru	: Sō desu ka. A, sorekara, kono hen ni (2) <u>ATM</u> arimasu ka.
女の人	：そうですね……。あ、(3)<u>コンビニ</u>にありますよ。	Onna no hito	: Sō desu ne....... . A, (2) <u>kombini</u> ni arimasu yo.
クマール	：(3)<u>コンビニ</u>はどこですか。	Kumāru	: (3) <u>Kombini</u> wa doko desu ka.
女の人	：(4)<u>さくら公園</u>の前です。	Onna no hito	: (4) <u>Sakura kōen</u> no mae desu.
クマール	：ありがとうございます。	Kumāru	: Arigatō gozaimasu.

---

①
(1) ふじ病院　　　　Fuji byōin
(2) 花屋　　　　　　hana-ya
(3) スーパー　　　　sūpā
(4) 病院の近く　　　byōin no chikaku

---

②
(1) 現代美術館　　　Gendai bijutsukan (=Modern art museum)
(2) コインロッカー　koin rokkā
(3) 地下鉄の駅　　　chikatetsu no eki
(4) バス停のむこう　basu-tei no mukō

MEMO

それから／sorekara／and (Used when uttering an additional statement or question.)

32

Material

Look at the map while doing the practice conversation on the left page.

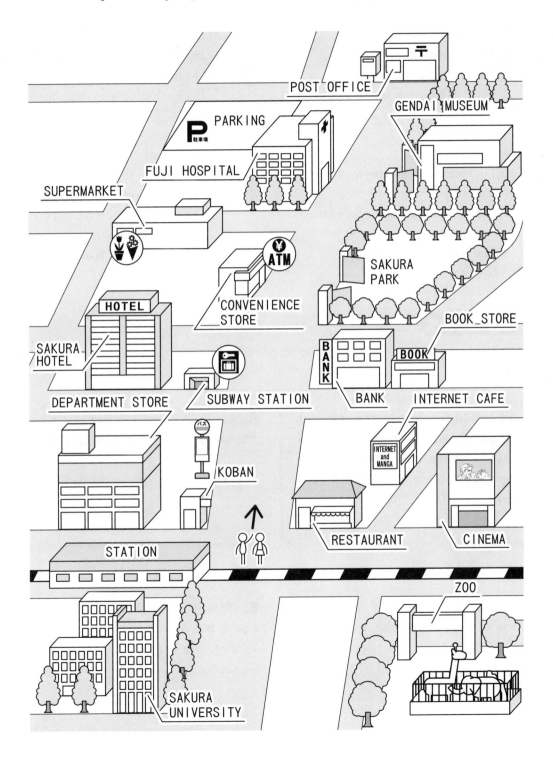

Listening

Listen to the conversation between the man and woman and choose the correct answer.

Q1 On the street

1. The internet café is over there.
2. The internet café is right here.
3. There internet café is straight down here.

Q2 At a supermarket

1. The customer is looking for a restroom.
2. The customer is looking for a cash register.
3. The customer is looking for a bookstore.

Q3 At a department store

1. The book store is on the third floor.
2. The book store is on the second floor.
3. The book store is on the ground floor.

Q4 On the street

1. The 100-yen store is in front of the convenience store.
2. The 100-yen store is behind the convenience store.
3. The 100-yen store is next to the convenience store.

Role playing

Role play using the cards below.   →See the map on page 33.

1.

> **A:** You would like to use the internet. You come across B-san in the street and ask if there is an internet café in the area, where it is, and if it is nearby.

> **B:** A-san stops to ask you questions in the street. Answer A-san's questions.

2.

> **A:** You are in front of the train station and want to take the bus to the Gendai Museum. Ask nearby B-san where the bus stop is and if it goes to the museum.

> **B:** This is your first time here. You saw a bus stop nearby, but you're not sure if the bus goes to the Gendai Museum.

Do you remember?

Use the phrases you have studied in this unit in situations ①–③ below.

①

②

③

Unit Phrases

● このへんに、ATM ありますか。   Kono hen ni, ATM arimasuka.   Is there an ATM around here?

● トイレ、どこですか。   Toire, doko desu ka.   Where is the restroom?

● 郵便局に行きたいんですが……。
ゆうびんきょく　い   Yūbinkyoku ni ikitai n desu ga....... .   I'm trying to go to the post office.

Useful expressions

● じゃ、いいです。   Ja, ii desu.   That's alright.

● もう一度いいですか。
いち ど   Mō ichido ii desu ka.   Would you say that one more time?

● ～は何階ですか。
なんかい   ...wa nan-kai desu ka.   What floor is the ... on?

● 近いですか。
ちか   Chikai desu ka.   Is it near here?

● それから、～   sorekara, …   and [Used when uttering an additional statement or question.]

Check!

Now I can...

☐ Ask if the store or place I want to go to is in the nearby area

☐ Ask for the location of the store or place I want to go to

☐ Ask and understand simple directions

How much is this?

これ、いくらですか。

Kore, ikura desu ka.

Shopping

買い物

GOALS FOR UNIT 3

- Ask if a store has what you are looking for

- Ask for the price of something you want to buy

- Request what you would like from a store

Phrase 1　Ask if a store has what you want to buy.

かさ、**ありますか。**

Kasa, **arimasu ka.**　　　　　　　　　**Do you have umbrellas?**

Track 17

> <u>NOTE</u>　"___ (wa) arimasu ka." was introduced as a way to ask if something exists in Unit 2. It can also mean "**Do you have____?**" → *See p.170, Grammar*

Ex.

ジョン　：すみません。<u>かさ</u>**(は) ありますか。**

店員　：はい、あります。こちらです。
てんいん

Jon　　：Sumimasen. <u>Kasa</u> **(wa) arimasu ka.**
Ten'in　：Hai, arimasu. Kochira desu.

> John　：Excuse me, do you have umbrellas?
> Clerk　：Yes, we do. They're right here.

Practice A

___、ありますか。
Use the following words with the phrase "____ , **arimasu ka?**"

かさ kasa umbrella	英語の新聞 えいご　しんぶん Eigo no shimbun English newspaper	国際電話のカード こくさいでんわ kokusai-denwa no kādo international calling card
地図 ちず chizu map	(お*)水 みず (o)mizu water	(お*)酒 さけ (o)sake alcoholic drink/Japanese sake
電池 でんち denchi battery	たばこ tabako cigarette	頭痛薬 ずつうやく zutsū-yaku headache medicine 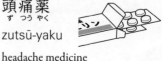

＊ The prefix "o-" makes nouns more polite. → See p.183, Grammar

B Put the words from A in <   > to complete the conversation exercise.

① ··

ジョン：すみません。〈かさ〉、ありますか。

店員：はい、こちらです。
てんいん

ジョン：ありがとうございます。

Jon　　: Sumimasen. <Kasa>, arimasu ka.

Ten'in　: Hai, kochira desu.

Jon　　: Arigatō gozaimasu.

John　: Excuse me. Do you have umbrellas ?

Clerk　: Yes. They're right here.

John　: Thank you.

② ··

ジョン：すみません。〈英語の新聞〉、ありますか。
　　　　　　　　えいご　しんぶん

店員：申し訳ありません。〈英語の新聞〉は、ないんです。
てんいん　もう　わけ　　　　えいご　しんぶん

ジョン：わかりました。

Jon　　: Sumimasen. < Eigo no shimbun >,
　　　　　arimasu ka.

Ten'in　: Mōshiwake arimasen.
　　　　　< Eigo no shimbun > wa, naindesu.

Jon　　: Wakarimashita.

John　: Excuse me. Do you have
　　　　English newspaper ?

Clerk　: I'm sorry, but we don't [have any English
　　　　newspapers].

John　: Okay.

MEMO

申し訳ありません。／Mōshiwake arimasen. ／I'm sorry. ["I have no excuse"; extremely polite]
もう　わけ

ないんです。／Naindesu. ／"...n desu" can be used to make a negative answer softer.
"Naindesu" = "We don't have it".

Phrase 2 — Ask how much something costs.

これ、いくらですか。

Kore, ikura desu ka?

How much is this?

Track 18

NOTE "Ikura" means "how much." "___ (wa) ikura desu ka?" means "How much is ___?" and is used to ask how much something costs.

Ex.

ジョン ：<u>これ</u>（は）いくらですか。

店員　：500円です。
てんいん　ごひゃくえん

Jon　　：<u>Kore</u> **(wa) ikura desu ka.**
Ten'in　： 500 [gohyaku]-en desu.

John　： How much is this?
Clerk　： It's 500 yen.

 A-1

___、いくらですか。

Let's use the following words with the phrase "___ , ikura desu ka?"

これ	それ	あれ
kore	sore	are
this	that / it	that

Speaker　Listener

Speaker　Listener

Speaker　Listener

---

* Please see **Demonstratives** on p.170 of **Grammar**.

A-2 Study the numbers from 10 to 10,000 (→see p. 47) and say the following prices in (1) – (7) with the phrase **"____-en desu."**

(1) ￥55   (2) ￥99   (3) ￥270   (4) ￥360   (5) ￥890   (6) ￥1,500   (7) ￥2,700

B Practice talking about prices with the pictures below.

ジョン ：すみません。〈ノート〉、いくらですか。

店員　：〈90円〉です。
てんいん　　　えん

Jon　　 : Sumimasen. < Nōto >, ikura desu ka.
Ten'in　: < 90-en > desu.

John　 : Excuse me. How much is this notebook?
Clerk　: It's 90 yen.

Ex. ノート
nōto
notebook
￥90

① ペン
pen
pen
￥120

② お弁当
べんとう
o-bentō
bento-box
￥550

③ タオル
taoru
towel
￥680

④ 時計
とけい
tokei
clock
￥1,980

⑤ バッグ
／かばん
baggu/kaban
bag
￥3,600

⑥ マフラー
mafurā
scarf
￥4,300

⑦ くつ
kutsu
shoes
￥8,800

Phrase 3 — Make a purchase.

このTシャツ、ください。

Kono T-shatsu, **kudasai.**　　　　**I'll have** this T-shirt.

NOTE　"___(o) kudasai." means "**Please give me** ___." and is used when making a purchase. "**Kono**" is always used before a noun. "**Kore**" means "**this**" and is also used before "**kudasai**".

Ex.

① すみません。<u>このTシャツ</u>（を）ください。

② すみません。<u>これ</u>（を）<u>ふたつ</u>ください。

① Sumimasen. <u>Kono T-shatsu</u> **(o)** kudasai.
② Sumimasen. <u>Kore</u> **(o)** <u>futatsu</u> kudasai.

> John : Excuse me. I'll have this T-shirt.
> John : Excuse me. I'll have two of these.

 A-1　___、ください。
Use the following words with the phrase "___ , **kudasai.**"

このTシャツ	そのTシャツ	あのTシャツ
kono T-shatsu	sono T-shatsu	ano T-shatsu
this T-shirt	that T-shirt	that T-shirt
これ	それ	あれ
kore	sore	are
this	that/it	that

42

A-2 これ、＿＿＿ください。

Say how many of each item you want with the phrase **"Kore, ＿＿＿ kudasai."**

ひとつ	ふたつ	みっつ	よっつ
hitotsu	futatsu	mittsu	yottsu
one	two	three	four

* 5 = itsutsu, 6 = muttsu, 7 = nanatsu, 8 = yattsu, 9 = kokonotsu, 10 = tō

Saying the number word with "ko" can also be used to count objects. → *See p.178, Grammar*

B Put the words from Practice A-1 and A-2 into < > to complete the conversation below.

ジョン ：すみません。^{A-1}＜このＴシャツ＞、^{A-2}＜ふたつ＞ください。

店員 ：はい。ありがとうございます。
てんいん

ジョン ：あ、それから、^{A-1}＜これ＞もください。

店員 ：かしこまりました。
てんいん

ジョン ：カードでお願いします。*
　　　　　　　　ねが

店員 ：お支払い方法は？
てんいん　　しはら　ほうほう

ジョン ：一回で。
　　　　いっかい

> * It is usually paid by cash if neither you nor the shop staff say anything about the way of the payment.

Jon : Sumimasen. ^{A-1}< Kono T-shatsu >,
^{A-2}< futatsu > kudasai.

Ten'in : Hai. Arigatō gozaimasu.

Jon : A, sorekara, ^{A-1}< kore > mo kudasai.

Ten'in : Kashikomari mashita.

Jon : Kādo de onegai shimasu.*

Ten'in : Oshiharai hōhō wa?

Jon : Ikkai de.

John	: Excuse me, I'll have two of these T-shirts.
Clerk	: Okay. Thank you.
John	: And I'll take this, too.
Clerk	: Alright.
John	: I'd like to pay by credit card.*
Clerk	: How many payments would you like to make?
John	: One, please.

MEMO

それから、〜もください。／Sorekara … mo kudasai.／And I'll have …. too.

カードでお願いします。／Kādo de onegaishimasu.／I'd like to pay by credit card.
　　　ねが

お支払い方法は？／Oshiharai hōhō wa?／How many payments will you make? ["What is your
しはら　ほうほう
payment method?"]

一回で。／Ikkai de.／One/Once, please.
いっかい

Phrase 4　Making requests at a store.

もうちょっと安いの、ありませんか。
やす

Mō chotto yasui **no, arimasen ka.**　Do you have one a little cheaper?

Track
20

NOTE　"Mō chotto" means "a little more" and can be used with adjectives. **"Mō chotto ____ no arimasen ka"** is often used to make a request while shopping. Although **"arimasen ka"** can also be used in the affirmative, is considered more polite to ask with a negative form.

Ex.

ジョン　：もうちょっと安いの（は）ありませんか。
　　　　　　　　　　やす

店員　　：こちらはいかがですか。
てんいん

Jon　　　: **Mō chotto** yasui **no (wa) arimasen ka.**

Ten'in　: Kochira wa ikaga desu ka.

> John　　: Do you have one a little
> 　　　　　 cheaper?
> Clerk　 : How about this one?

Practice
A

もうちょっと＿＿＿の、ありませんか。

Let's use the following words with the phrase **"Mō chotto ____ no, arimasen ka."**

安い やす yasui cheap	大きい おお ōkii big	小さい ちい chiisai small	軽い かる karui light/light weight
長い なが nagai long	短い みじか mijikai short	他のメーカー* ほか hoka no mēkā another makers	他の色* ほか　いろ hoka no iro another colors → *See Appendix, Colors*

＊ You don't use "mō chotto" with "hoka no" (another, the other)

B-1 Put the words from Practice A in <   > and practice the conversation below.

-Looking at something in a shop-

ジョン ：すみません。これ、もうちょっと〈安い〉の、ありませんか。
　　　　　　　　　　　　　　　　　　　やす

店員 ：すみません。これだけなんです。
てんいん

ジョン ：そうですか。じゃあ、ちょっと考えます。
　　　　　　　　　　　　　　　　　　　かんが

Jon	: Sumimasen. Kore, mō chotto	John	: Excuse me. Do you have a cheaper one of
	< yasui >no arimasen ka.		these?
Ten'in	: Sumimasen. Kore dakenan desu.	Clerk	: I'm sorry, this is all we have.
Jon	: Sō desu ka. Jā, chotto kangaemasu.	John	: Okay, I'll think about it then.

 B-2 Study the numbers from 10 to 100,000 (p. 47) and practice the conversation with the words below.

ジョン ：すみません。この〈自転車〉、いくらですか。
　　　　　　　　　　　　じ てんしゃ

店員 ：〈10980〉円です。
てんいん　　　　　　　　えん

Jon	: Sumimasen. Kono <jitensha>, ikura	John	: Excuse me. How much is this <bicycle>?
	desu ka.	Clerk	: It's <10,980> yen.
Ten'in	: <10980> -en desu.		

Ex. 自転車　　　① 携帯　　　② 電子辞書　　　③ パソコン
　　 じ てん しゃ　　　　けい たい　　　　でん し じ しょ

jitensha　　　　keitai　　　　denshi-jisho　　　　pasokon

bicycle　　　cellular phone　　　electronic dictionary　　　personal computer

¥10,980　　　¥26,000　　　¥47,000　　　¥98,000

MEMO

こちらはいかがですか。／Kochira wa ikaga desuka.／How about this one?

これだけなんです。／Kore dake nandesu.／This is all we have.

じゃあ、ちょっと考えます。／Jā, chotto kangaemasu.／I'll think about it then.
　　　　　　　　かんが

Dialogue

Look at the picture on the right page and have a practice conversation replacing the words in (1) – (5).

ジョン　：すみません。

　　　　(1)Tシャツ、ありますか。

店員　：はい、ございます。こちらです。

ジョン　：それはいくらですか。

店員　：(2)3900円です。

ジョン　：(3)もうちょっと安いの、

　　　　ありませんか。

店員　：(4)こちらは1980円です。

ジョン　：じゃあ、(5)それ、みっつください。

店員　：ありがとうございます。

Jon　：Sumimasen.

　　　①T-shatsu, arimasu ka.

Ten'in　：Hai, gozaimasu. Kochira desu.

Jon　：Sore wa ikura desu ka.

Ten'in　：(2) 3900-en desu.

Jon　：(3) Mō chotto yasui no,

　　　arimasen ka.

Ten'in　：(4) Kochira wa 1980-en desu.

Jon　：Jā, (5) sore, mittsu kudasai.

Ten'in　：Arigatō gozaimasu.

① (1) 水　　　　　　　　　　mizu
　(2) 150円　　　　　　　　　150-en
　(3) もうちょっと小さいの　Mō chotto chiisai no
　(4) こちらは100円です　　Kochira wa 100-en desu
　(5) それ、ひとつ　　　　　sore, hitotsu

② (1) デジカメ　　　　　　　dejikame
　(2) 29800円　　　　　　　29800-en
　(3) 他の色の　　　　　　　Hoka no iro no
　(4) 青いのと黒いのがあります　Aoi no to kuroi no ga arimasu
　(5) 黒いの　　　　　　　　kuroi no

MEMO

ございます。／Gozaimasu.／[A politer way to say "arimasu (=have)"]

46

Material

1 Look at the pictures below and complete the practice conversation on the left page.

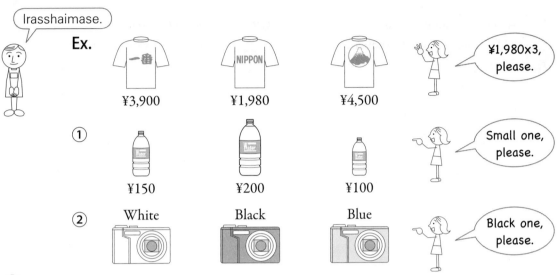

Irasshaimase.

Ex.

¥3,900　　¥1,980　　¥4,500

¥1,980×3, please.

① ¥150　　¥200　　¥100

Small one, please.

② White　　Black　　Blue

Black one, please.

2 Counting 1 – 100,000

1-10	11-20	10-100	100-1,000	1,000-10,000	10,000-100,000
1 ichi	11 jū-ichi	10 jū	100 hyaku	1,000 sen	10,000 ichi-man
2 ni	12 jū-ni	20 ni-jū	200 ni-hyaku	2,000 ni-sen	20,000 ni-man
3 san	13 jū-san	30 san-jū	**300** **sambyaku**	3,000 san-zen	30,000 sam-man
4 yon/shi	14 jū-yon	40 yon-jū	400 yon-hyaku	4,000 yon-sen	40,000 yon-man
5 go	15 jū-go	50 go-jū	500 go-hyaku	5,000 go-sen	50,000 go-man
6 roku	16 jū-roku	60 roku-jū	**600** **roppyaku**	6,000 roku-sen	60,000 roku-man
7 nana/shichi	17 jū-nana	70 nana-jū	700 nana-hyaku	7,000 nana-sen	70,000 nana-man
8 hachi	18 jū-hachi	80 hachi-jū	**800** **happyaku**	**8,000** **hassen**	80,000 hachi-man
9 kyū/ku	19 jū-kyū	90 kyū-jū	900 kyū-hyaku	9,000 kyū-sen	90,000 kyū-man
10 jū	20 ni-jū	100 hyaku	1,000 sen	10,000 ichi-man	100,000 jū-man

Listening

Listen to the conversation between the man and woman and choose the correct answer.

Q1 At a convenience store

1. They don't have newspapers.
2. They have cigarettes.
3. They don't have cigarettes.

Q2 At a kiosk

1. The umbrella is 400 yen.
2. The umbrella is 600 yen.
3. The umbrella is 800 yen.

Q3 Inside a *shinkansen*

1. The man wants a bento box.
2. The man wants 2 bento boxes.
3. The man wants 3 bento boxes.

Q4 At a department store

1. The woman wants a bigger one.
2. The woman wants a cheaper one.
3. The woman wants a smaller one.

Role playing

Role play using the cards below.

1. At an electronics store

A: You are at an electronics store. Ask if they have a battery charger (jūdenki) for your cellular phone, how much it costs, and if they have one that costs less.

B: You are a clerk at an electronics store. The store has chargers for 1,000 and 1,500 yen. If asked about prices, first recommend the more expensive model.

2. At a bookstore

A: You are at a bookstore and want to buy a map of Tokyo. Ask the clerk for a Tokyo map, how much it is, and if they have any bigger ones. You will also need a receipt.

B: You work at a bookstore. The store has a small map for 500 yen and big map for 800 yen. If asked, first recommend the smaller map.

Do you remember?

Use the phrases you have studied in this unit in situations ①–④ below.

Phrases for This Unit

Unit Phrases

- かさ、ありますか。 | Kasa, arimasu ka? | Do you have umbrellas?
- これ、いくらですか。 | Kasa, ikura desu ka? | How much is this?
- このＴシャツ、ください。 | Kono T-shatsu, kudasai. | I'll have this T-shirt.
- もうちょっと安いの、ありませんか。 | Mō chotto yasui no, arimasen ka. | Do you have one a little cheaper?

Useful expressions

- ちょっと考えます。 | Chotto kangaemasu. | I will think about it.
- お支払い方法は？ — 一回で。 | O-shiharai hōhō wa? — Ikkai de. | How many payments would you like to make? — One.
- それから、これもください。 | Sorekara, kore mo kudasai. | I'll take this, too.

Check!

Now I can...

- ☐ Ask if a store has what I am looking for
- ☐ Ask for the price of something I want to buy
- ☐ Request what I would like from a store

Take out, please.

持ち帰りで。
Mochikaeri de.

Convenience stores and restaurants
コンビニ・レストラン

GOALS FOR UNIT 4

- Make orders at restaurants

- Request and ask about items on the menu

- Communicate with people at convenience stores and restaurants

Phrase 1 — Make a request at a restaurant.

メニュー、お願_{ねが}いします。

Menyū, **onegaishimasu.**

Could I have a menu?

Track 26

> **NOTE** "[Noun] (o) onegaishimasu" is used when ordering food and making a request to receive something or have something done. A counter word can optionally come after the noun. → *See p.43 and p.178, Counters*

Ex.

① すみません。<u>メニュー</u>（を）お願_{ねが}いします。

② <u>カレー</u>（を）ひとつ、お願_{ねが}いします。

① Sumimasen. <u>Menyū</u> **(o) onegaishimasu.**

② <u>Karē</u> **(o)** hitotsu, **onegaishimasu.**

> ① Excuse me. Could I have a menu?
> ② One curry, please.

Practice A-1

_____、お願_{ねが}いします。

Use the following words with the phrase "____ , **onegaishimasu.**"

メニュー	注文 ちゅうもん	おしぼり
menyū	chūmon	oshibori
menu	order	rolled wet towel [used to wash one's hands]
取り皿 と　さら	これと同じの おな	グラス
torizara	kore to onaji no	gurasu
small plate	the same as this	glass
スプーン／フォーク	カレー	生ビール なま
supūn / fōku	karē	nama bīru
spoon / fork	curry with rice → *See Appendix, Food*	draft beer → *See Appendix, Drinks*

A-2 Ask for words in Practice A-1 in the quantities below.

ひとつ	ふたつ	みっつ	よっつ
hitotsu	futatsu	mittsu	yottsu
one	two	three	four

* Please see **Counters** on p.178 of **Grammar** for numbers greater than 4.

B Put the words from Practice A-1 and A-2 into <　　> to complete the conversation below.

店員　：ご注文、お決まりですか。
ジョン：はい。^{A-1}〈カレー〉^{A-2}〈ひとつ〉と ^{A-1}〈生ビール〉^{A-2}〈ひとつ〉、お願いします。
店員　：以上でよろしいですか。
ジョン：はい、以上で。あ、あとお水もらえますか。
店員　：かしこまりました。

Ten'in : Go-chūmon, o-kimari desu ka.
Jon　 : Hai. <Karē><hitotsu> to
　　　　<nama bīru><hitotsu>, onegaishimasu.
Ten'in : Ijō de yoroshii desu ka.
Jon　 : Hai, ijō de. A, ato o-mizu moraemasu ka.
Ten'in : Kashikomarimashita.

Waiter : Are you ready to order?
John　 : Yes. I'll have one curry and one draft beer, please.
Waiter : Will that be all for you?
John　 : Yes, that's all. Oh, could I also have some water?
Waiter : Right away.

MEMO

(ご注文)お決まりですか。／(Go-chūmon) o-kimari desu ka. ／Are you ready to order?

以上で。／Ijō de. ／That's all.

あと～／ato... ／and...

～もらえますか。／... moraemasu ka? ／Could I have ....?

かしこまりました。／Kashikomarimashita. ／Certainly/Yes/Right away.

Phrase 2 — Ask about things you don't understand or don't know about.

今日のランチ、**なんですか。**
きょう

Kyō no ranchi, **nan desu ka.**   **What's the lunch of the day?**

Track
27

NOTE "Nan" means "what." " ___(wa) nan desu ka" means "What is ___ ?"

Ex.

ジョン ：すみません。<u>今日のランチ</u>（は）**なんですか。**
　　　　　　　　きょう

店員　：カレーです。
てんいん

Jon　　: Sumimasen. <u>Kyō no ranchi</u> **(wa)**
　　　　　　nan desu ka.

Ten-in : Karē desu.

John　　: Excuse me, what's the lunch of the day?
Waiter　: Curry.

Practice
A

　　　　　、**なんですか。**
Use the following words with the phrase "_____ , **nan desu ka.**"

今日のランチ きょう kyō no ranchi lunch of the day	日替わり* ひ が higawari meal of the day	おすすめ osusume recommendation
これ kore this	あれ are that	デザート dezāto dessert
セットのドリンク setto no dorinku included drink	この〈白い・黒い・赤い〉の しろ　　くろ　　あか kono <shiroi / kuroi / akai > no this <white / black / red > one → *See Appendix, Colors*	

＊ **Higawari** ["day change"] originally comes from the practice of restaurants offering a different meal each day. Restaurants now offer special menus each day, such as daily set meals and lunches, which are referred to as **higawari**.

 Using the menu on page 61, put the words from Practice A into < > and complete the conversation.

ジョン ：〈今日のランチ〉、なんですか。
　　　　きょう
店員 ：〈カレー〉です。
てんいん

John　　 : < Kyō no ranchi >, nan desu ka.
Ten'in　 :< Karē > desu.

> John　　: What's the lunch of the day?
> Waiter : Curry and rice.

 Look at the Pre-text and ask questions about items on the menu using the template below.

ジョン ：すみません。これ、なんですか。

店員 ：〈牛丼〉です。
てんいん　ぎゅうどん
ジョン ：この〈赤い〉の、なんですか。
　　　　　あか
店員 ：〈しょうが〉ですよ。
てんいん
ジョン ：〈しょうが〉？ 〈しょうが〉って、なんですか？

店員 ：〈Ginger〉です。
てんいん

Jon　　 : Sumimasen. Kore, nan desu ka.
Ten'in　 : < Gyūdon > desu.
Jon　　 : Kono < akai > no, nan desu ka.
Ten'in　 : < Shōga > desu yo.
Jon　　 : < Shōga > ? < Shōga > tte, nan desu ka.
Ten'in　 : < Ginger > desu.

> John　　: Excuse me. What is this?
> Waiter : It's gyu-don.
> John　　: What is this red stuff?
> Waiter : That's shoga.
> John　　: Shoga? What is shoga?
> Waiter : It's ginger.

MEMO

〜って、なんですか。／ ...tte nan desu ka. ／ What is ...? [Used to ask about the meaning of a word or something you do not understand.]

Phrase 3 — Choose an option and then explain it in a natural-sounding way.

持ち帰りで。
もかえ

Mochikaeri **de.**

Take out**, please.**

Track
28

NOTE Use **"de"** when choosing from a series of options. Saying **"____de onegai shimasu"** is more polite.

Ex.

店員　：こちらでお召し上がりですか。
てんいん　　　　　　　　め　あ

ジョン：いいえ、<u>持ち帰り</u>で。
　　　　　　　　　も　かえ

Ten'in　: Kochira de omeshiagari desu ka.

Jon　　: Iie, <u>mochikaeri</u> **de.**

> Staff　: Would you like to eat in?
> John　: No, take out, please.

Practice
A

____で。

Use the following words with the phrase **"____ de."**, when asked the question below.

Q.　Would you like to eat in?

ここ／店内 てんない koko / tennai here / eat in	持ち帰り もかえ mochikaeri take out

Q.　That comes hot or cold.

ホット hotto hot (drink)	アイス aisu iced (drink)

Q.　What size would you like?

エス／エム／エル

esu / emu / eru

small / medium / large

Q.　Would you like a bag?/Would you like these in separate bags?

そのまま sonomama The way it is 	一緒* いっしょ issho together	別々* べつべつ betsu betsu separate

* **"issho"** (together), **"betsu betsu"** (separate) [also used when determining how many bills are necessary]

56

B-1 Practice ordering with the menu below.

店員：いらっしゃいませ。こちらでお召し上がりですか。
ジョン：はい、ここで。／いいえ、持ち帰りで。
店員：ご注文をどうぞ。
ジョン：〈チーズバーガー〉と〈コーラ〉、お願いします。
店員：〈コーラ〉のサイズは？
ジョン：〈エム〉で。

Ten'in : Irasshaimase. Kochira de omeshiagari desu ka.	Staff : Welcome. Would you like to eat in?
Jon : Hai, koko de. / Iie, mochikaeri de.	John : Yes. / No, take out, please.
Ten'in : Go-chūmon o dōzo.	Staff : May I take your order?
Jon : < Chīzu bāgā> to < kōra >, onegai shimasu.	John : I'll have a cheeseburger and a cola, please.
Ten'in : < Kōra > no saizu wa?	Staff : What size cola would you like?
Jon : < Emu > de.	John : Medium, please.

～MENU～

Burger
 Hamburger
 Cheese burger
 Teriyaki Burger

Drink
Cola
Iced coffee
Iced tea

Side Menu
 French fries
 Salad

B-2 Make your own conversation using the words in Practice A.

 MEMO
いらっしゃいませ。／Irasshaimase.／Welcome. /May I help you?

こちらでお召し上がりですか。／Kochira de omeshiagari desu ka.／Would you like to eat in?

ご注文をどうぞ。／Go-chūmon o dōzo.／May I take your order?

Politely refuse unnecessary things.

袋、けっこうです。
ふくろ

Fukuro, **kekkō desu.**　　　　　No bag, thank you.

Track
29

NOTE **"Kekkō desu."** can be used to say **"No thank you."** and is a polite way to refuse things.

Ex.

ジョン : 袋(は)けっこうです。
　　　 ふくろ

店員　 : かしこまりました。
てんいん

Jon　　 : Fukuro **(wa) kekkō desu.**

Ten'in : Kashikomarimashita.

John　 : No bag, thank you.
Clerk　 : Okay.

Practice
A

＿＿＿、けっこうです。

Let's use the following words with the phrase "＿＿＿ , **kekkō desu.**

袋 ふくろ fukuro bag	紙袋 かみ ぶくろ kami- bukuro paper bag	ビニール袋 ぶくろ biniru-bukuro plastic bag	レシート reshīto receipt
(お)はし (o)hashi chopsticks	スプーン／フォーク supūn / fōku spoon / fork		ストロー sutorō straw
ミルク miruku cream	砂糖 さ とう satō sugar		ガムシロップ gamu shiroppu liquid sugar

B-1 Put the words from Practice A in <　　> and practice the conversation below.

店員　　：〈袋〉、ご利用ですか。
　てんいん　　ふくろ　　りょう
ジョン：いいえ、けっこうです。／はい、お願いします。
　　　　　　　　　　　　　　　　　　ねが

Ten'in　：< Fukuro > go-riyō desu ka.
Jon　　：Iie, kekkō desu. / Hai, onegaishimasu.

┌─────────────────────────────────────┐
│ Clerk　：Would you like a bag?   │
│ John　：No, thank you. / Yes, please.│
└─────────────────────────────────────┘

 B-2 Look at the picture below and tell the shop staff what you don't need.

ジョン：あ、<　　　　　>、けっこうです。

店員　　：かしこまりました。
　てんいん

Jon　　：a, <　　> kekkō desu.
Ten'in　：kashikomarimashita.

┌─────────────────────────────────────┐
│ John　：Oh, I don't need a _____. │
│ Clerk　：Okay.   │
└─────────────────────────────────────┘

① 　② 　③ 　④

MEMO

～、ご利用ですか。／ ..., go-riyō desu ka. ／ Would you like to use...? [polite expression]
　　　りょう

Dialogue

Look at the menu on page 61 and have a practice conversation replacing the words in (1)-(4), then make your own conversation.

店員 てんいん :ご注文、お決まりですか。 ちゅうもん き	Ten'in : Go-chūmon, okimari desu ka.
ジョン :おすすめはなんですか。	Jon : Osusume wa nan desu ka.
店員 てんいん :(1)今日のランチです。 きょう	Ten'in : (1) Kyō no ranchi desu.
ジョン :じゃあ、それ(2)ひとつ、お願いします。 ねが	Jon : Jā, sore (2) hitotsu, onegaishimasu.
店員 てんいん :お飲み物は？ の もの	Ten'in : O-nomimono wa?
ジョン :(3)コーラで。	Jon : (3) Kōra de.
店員 てんいん :ご一緒にデザートはいかがですか。 いっしょ	Ten'in : Go-issho ni dezāto wa ikaga desu ka.
ジョン :けっこうです。	Jon : Kekkō desu.
-During a meal-	～During a meal～
ジョン :すみません。(4)お水もらえますか。 みず	Jon : Sumimasen.(4) O-mizu moraemasu ka.

---

① (1) パスタランチ — pasuta ranchi
(2) ふたつ — futatsu
(3) 生ビール — nama-bīru
なま
(4) おしぼり — oshibori

---

② (1) 日替わり定食 — higawari-tēshoku
ひ が ていしょく
(2) みっつ — mittsu
(3) アイスコーヒー — aisu-kōhī
(4) ストロー — sutorō

---

③ Make your own conversation

MEMO

ご注文お決まりですか。／Go-chūmon, o-kimari desu ka／Are you ready to order?
ちゅうもん き

(お)飲み物／(o)nomimono／beverage
の もの

ご一緒に～はいかがですか。／Go-issho ni...wa ikaga desu ka.／Would you like ...with that?
いっしょ

Material

Look at the picture below and practice the conversation on the left page.

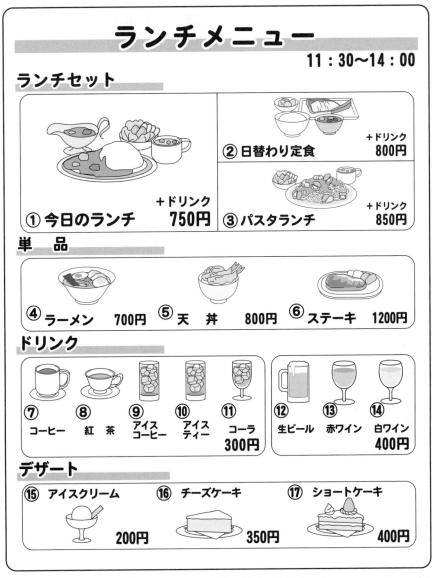

① 今日のランチ／kyō no ranchi／Lunch of the day　②日替わり定食／higawari-tēshoku／Today's set meal
③ パスタランチ／pasuta ranchi／Pasta lunch　④ ラーメン／rāmen／Ramen
⑤ 天丼／ten-don／Tendon　⑥ ステーキ／sutēki／Steak　⑦ コーヒー／kōhī／Coffee
⑧ 紅茶／kōcha／Black tea　⑨ アイスコーヒー／aisu-kōhī／Iced coffee
⑩ アイスティー／aisu-thī／Iced tea　⑪ コーラ／kōra／Cola　⑫ 生ビール／nama-bīru／Draft beer
⑬ 赤ワイン／aka-wain／Red wine　⑭ 白ワイン／shiro-wain／White wine
⑮ アイスクリーム／aisu-kurīmu／Ice cream　⑯ チーズケーキ／chīzu-keki／Cheesecake
⑰ ショートケーキ／shōto-kēki／Strawberry shortcake

Listen to the conversation between the man and woman and choose the correct answer.

Q1 At a sushi restaurant

1. The waiter does not have any recommendations.
2. The customer asked about the lunch of the day.
3. The customer asked for a recommendation.

Q3 A waiter at an izakaya comes to take away an empty glass

1. The customer orders another glass of draft beer.
2. The customer asks for a glass of water.
3. The customer asks for another plate.

Q2 At a fast food restaurant

1. The customer got cream.
2. The customer got liquid sugar.
3. The customer got both cream and liquid sugar.

Q4 Checking out at a restaurant

1. The customers paid together.
2. The customers paid separately.
3. The customers received separate receipts.

Role playing

Role play using the cards below.

1.

A: You are a customer at a restaurant. Call the waiter and ask for a menu, then order what you would like to eat.

B: You are part of the wait staff at a restaurant. Using the menu on page 61, take A-san's order and ask if he/she would like something to drink.

2.

A: You are talking to the cashier at a fast food restaurant. Make a take-out order for one hamburger and one iced coffee.

B: You are the cashier at a fast food restaurant. Take A-san's order, ask if he/she would like milk and sugar with the iced coffee, and if you should put the items in separate bags.

Do you remember?

Use the phrases you have studied in this unit in situations ①–④ below.

Phrases For This Unit

Unit Phrases

- メニュー、お願いします。
  Menyū, omegaishimasu.
  Could I have a menu?

- 今日のランチ、なんですか。
  Kyō no ranchi, nan desu ka.
  What's the lunch of the day?

- 持ち帰りで。
  Mochikaeri de.
  Take out, please.

- 袋、けっこうです。
  Fukuro, kekkō desu.
  No bag, thank you.

Useful expressions

- ～ってなんですか。
  ...tte nan desu ka?
  What is ...? [Used to ask about the meaning of a word or something you do not understand.]

- ～、ご利用ですか。
  ... go-riyō desu ka.
  Will you be using ...? [Polite expression]

- 以上で。
  Ijō de.
  That's all.

- ～はいかがですか。
  ... wa ikaga desu ka.
  Would you like ...?

Check!

Now I can...

- ☐ Make orders at restaurants

- ☐ Request and ask about items on the menu

- ☐ Communicate with people at convenience stores and restaurants

One More Step

● Useful expressions at restaurants

1. Entering a restaurant

(1) 店員 ：何名様ですか。

　　客 ：ひとりです。(ふたり、さんにん、よにん…)

　　Ten'in ： Nan-mei sama desuka.

　　Kyaku ： Hitori desu. [futari, san-nin, yo-nin …]

> Waiter : How many people?
> Customer : One. (Two, three, four, etc.)

(2) 店員 ：おたばこは？

　　客 ：① 吸います。／喫煙席お願いします。

　　　　② 吸いません。／禁煙席お願いします。

　　Ten'in ： O-tabako wa?

　　Kyaku ： ① Suimasu. / Kitsuen-seki onegaishimasu.
　　　　　 ② Suimasen. / Kin'en-seki onegaishimasu.

> Waiter : Do you smoke?
> Customer : ① Yes. / Smoking, please.
> ② No. / Non-smoking, please.

(3) 店員 ：すみません。ただいま満席です。

　　客 ：どのぐらい待ちますか。

　　店員 ：15分ぐらいです。

　　Ten'in ： Sumimasen, tadaima man-seki desu.

　　Kyaku ： Donogurai machimasu ka?

　　Ten'in ： Jūgo-fun gurai desu.

> Waiter : I'm sorry, but we're full right now.
> Customer : How long is the wait?
> Waiter : About 15 minutes.

2. Asking about food

(1) 客 ：これ、肉入ってますか。

　　店員 ：はい、入ってます。／いいえ、入ってません。

　　Kyaku ： Kore, <u>niku</u> haittemasu ka?

　　Ten'in ： Hai, haittemasu. / Iie, haittemasen.

> Customer : Is there <u>meat</u> in this?
> Waiter : Yes, there is. / No, there's not.

(2) 客 ：たまねぎ抜きで、お願いします。

　　Kyaku ： <u>Tamanegi</u> nuki de, onegaishimasu.

> Customer : Without <u>onions</u>, please.

3. Leaving a restaurant

(1) 客 : すみません。お会計、お願いします。
　　 店員 : お会計はご一緒でよろしいですか。
　　 客 : はい、一緒で。／いいえ、別々で。

　　 Kyaku : Sumimasen. O-kaikei, onegaishimasu..
　　 Ten'in : O-kaikei wa go-issho de yoroshii desu ka.
　　 Kyaku : Hai, issho de. / Iie, betsu betsu de.

> Customer : Excuse me, could I have the bill, please?
> Waiter : Will you pay together?
> Customer : Yes, together. / No, separately.

(2) 客 : ごちそうさまでした。おいしかったです。

　　 Kyaku : Gochisōsama deshita. Oishikatta desu.

> Customer : Thank you. It was delicious.

Good to Know

Japanese fast food - Keywords -

● 食券　shokken

Several restaurants in Japan, like **tachi-gui** (stand and eat) **soba** bars and **gyūdon** (beef rice bowl) counters, use a **shokken**, or food ticket, system. Upon entering a restaurant, customers purchase a **shokken** ticket for what they want to eat from an automated vending machine and hand it to a server, who exchanges it for food. After inserting money into a **shokken** machine, buttons featuring food you can buy for that amount of money light up. After pushing the lit up button for the food you want, be sure to hit the **otsuri** (change) button to receive your change.

● セルフサービス　serufu-sābisu

Several Japanese fast food restaurants are "self-service", meaning customers are responsible for retrieving their own water, seasonings, and condiments that are placed on most counters and tables. After customers finish eating, they dispose of their own garbage, and if a tray has been used, they return it to the tray collection counter.

● 並　nami・大盛　ōmori / 大　dai・中　chū・小　shō

Sometimes customers must specify the size of the dish they would like when ordering food, especially at **gyūdon** restaurants. Whereas the words **nami** (regular) and **ōmori** (large) are used to describe donburi dishes, restaurants like noodle houses use the terms **dai** (large), **chū** (regular), and **shō** (small). A typical order can be made by saying **"Gyūdon, nami de onegaishimasu."** (I'll have a regular beef rice bowl, please.) or **"Udon no dai, onegaishimasu."** (I'll have a large bowl of udon, please.)

Can I pay by credit card?

カードでいいですか。

Kādo de ii desu ka.

Asking permission

許可を得る

GOALS FOR UNIT 5

- Use simple sentences to ask for permission

- Confirm things to make sure documents are submitted smoothly

Phrase 1
Use nouns to ask for permission.

カードでいいですか。

Kādo de ii desu ka.

Can I pay by credit card?

Track
○
35

NOTE "[Noun] de ii desu ka." is used to ask for permission, and means "**Can I do something with/by [noun]?**" or "**Is [noun] okay?**"

Ex.

ジョン ：すみません。<u>カード</u>でいいですか。

店員 ：はい、だいじょうぶですよ。
てんいん

Jon ：Sumimasen, <u>kādo</u> **de ii desu ka.**

Ten'in ：Hai, daijōbu desu yo.

John ：Excuse me, can I pay by credit card?

Casher ：Yes, that's okay.

Practice A

_____ でいいですか

Use the following words with the phrase "_____**de ii desu ka?**"

カード	これ	一万円（札）
kādo	kore	いち まん えん さつ
(credit) card	this	ichiman-en (satsu)
		ten-thousand yen (note)

英語	ローマ字	今度
えい ご	じ	こん ど
Eigo	Rōma-ji	kondo
English	Roman letters	next time

あとで	予約なし	くつ
	よ やく	
atode	yoyaku nashi	kutsu
later	without a reservation	shoes

Practice
B

Use words from Practice A in < > to practice having a conversation.
*Choose words suitable for the situations in ②.

① ••

ジョン：すみません、〈カード〉でいいですか。

店員：ええ、いいですよ。／申し訳ありませんが、ちょっと……。
てんいん　　　　　　　　　　　　　　もう　わけ

Jon　　 : Sumimasen, < kādo > de ii desu ka.

Ten'in : Ee, ii desu yo.
　　　　 / Mōshiwake arimasen ga, chotto...... .

> John　　 : Excuse me, can I pay by credit card?
> Casher : Yes, that's fine.
> 　　　　　/ I'm terribly sorry, but [we don't accept
> 　　　　　credit cards].

② ••

1. Checking out at a store

店員　：980円です。
てんいん　　　　えん

ジョン：すみません、〈　　　　〉でいいですか。

Ten'in　 : 980-en desu.

Jon　　　 : Sumimasen, < > de ii desu ka.

> Casher : That comes to 980 yen.
> John　　 : Excuse me, could I use a _____ ?

2. Filling out an application

店員　：こちらにご記入ください。
てんいん　　　　　　き にゅう

ジョン：〈　　　　　　〉でいいですか。

Ten'in　 : Kochira ni go-kinyū kudasai.

Jon　　　 : < > de ii desu ka.

> Clerk　 : Please fill out [the form] here.
> John　　 : Can I use a _____ ? / Is _____ okey?

3. Entering a restaurant

店員　：いらっしゃいませ。
てんいん

ジョン：すみません、〈　　　　　　〉でいいですか。

Ten'in　 : Irasshaimase.

Jon　　　 : Sumimasen, < > de ii desu ka.

> Clerk　 : Welcome.
> John　　 : Excuse me, is _____ alright?

MEMO
いいですよ。／Ii desu yo.／That's fine.
こちらにご記入ください。／Kochira ni go-kinyū kudasai.／Please fill out (the form) here.
　　き にゅう
いらっしゃいませ。／Irasshaimase.／Welcome. / May I help you?

Phrase 2   Use verbs to ask for permission.

このペン、借りてもいいですか。
か

Kono pen, kari**te mo ii desu ka.**   **May I borrow this pen?**

Track
36

> NOTE   "[Verb-te] mo ii desu ka." is also used to ask for permission, and means "May/Can I [verb]?" → See Grammar p.173, Verb te-form

Ex.

ジョン　　　：すみません。このペン、借りてもいいですか。
　　　　　　　　　　　　　　　　　　　　か

受付の人：どうぞ。
うけつけ　ひと

Jon　　　　　　　　: Sumimasen. Kono pen,
　　　　　　　　　　　kari**te mo ii desu ka**.

Uketsuke no hito　: Dōzo.

John　　　　　: Excuse me. May I borrow this
　　　　　　　　　pen?
Receptionist : Yes.

Practice A

[Verb-te]もいいですか。
Use the following words with the phrase "__[Verb-te]__ mo ii desu ka."

借りて か karite borrow	見て み mite see/look/watch 	使って つか tsukatte use
入って はい haitte come in	座って すわ suwatte sit here	もらって moratte receive/have
たばこを吸って す tabako o sutte smoke	写真を撮って しゃ　しん　と shashin o totte take a picture	試着して し　ちゃく shichaku shite try on

Put the right word in < > and practice having a conversation. Several words may fit in the blanks.

① •

- At a temple -

ジョン　：すみません。ここ、〈　　　　　〉もいいですか。

係員　：はい、どうぞ。
かかりいん

ジョン　：あと、これ、〈　　　　　〉もいいですか。

係員　：ええ、いいですよ。
かかりいん

　　　　　／すみません。それはちょっと……。

Jon　　　　: Sumimasen. Koko, <　　　> mo ii desu ka.	John　　: Excuse me, can I _____ here?
Kakari-in : Hai, dōzo.	Staff　　: Yes.
Jon　　　　: Ato, kore, <　　>mo ii desu ka.	John　　: Also, could I _____ blank this?
Kakari-in : Ee,ii desu yo.	Staff　　: Yes, that's fine.
/ Sumimasen. Sore wa chotto…….	/ I'm sorry, but that's not allowed.

② •

- At the office -

ジョン　：このパソコン、〈　　　　　〉もいいですか。

田中　：今はちょっと……。
たなか　いま

ジョン　：じゃ、あとで〈　　　　　〉もいいですか。

田中　：はい、いいですよ。
たなか

Jon　　　　: Kono pasokon, <　　>mo ii desu ka.	John　　: Can I _____ this computer?
Tanaka　　: Ima wa chotto…….	Tanaka : Now's not a good time.
Jon　　　　: Ja, atode <　　>mo ii desu ka.	John　　: Okay, then could I _____ it later?
Tanaka　　: Hai, ii desu yo.	Tanaka : Yes, that's fine.

MEMO	
どうぞ。／Dōzo.／Please / Feel free.	
あと／ato／also	
それはちょっと……。／Sore wa chotto…….／I'm sorry but that's not allowed.	
今はちょっと……。／Ima wa chotto…….／Now's not a good time. いま	

71

Dialogue

Do tasks on the right page using the following conversation template and changing words (1) - (5).

ジョン :	すみません、 (1)<u>会員</u>になりたいんですが……。 _{かいいん}
店員 :	本日、身分証明書は _{てんいん ほんじつ み ぶんしょうめいしょ} お持ちですか。 _も
ジョン :	(2)<u>外国人登録証</u>でいいですか。 _{がいこくじんとうろくしょう}
店員 :	はい、けっこうです。 _{てんいん} それから、(3)<u>写真</u>はお持ちですか。 _{しゃしん も}
ジョン :	えっと、(4)<u>今度</u>でいいですか。 _{こん ど}
店員 :	はい、だいじょうぶです。 _{てんいん} では、こちらにご記入ください。 _{き にゅう}
ジョン :	(5)<u>このペン、借りて</u>もいいですか。 _か
店員 :	ええ、いいですよ。 _{てんいん}

Jon :	Sumimasen,
	(1)<u>Kai-in ni naritai</u> n desu ga...... .
Ten'in :	Honjitsu, mibun shōmei sho wa
	o-mochi desu ka.
Jon :	(2)<u>Gaikoku-jin tōroku shō</u> de ii desu ka.
Ten'in :	Hai, kekkō desu.
	Sorekara, (3)<u>shashin</u> wa o-mochi desu ka.
Jon :	Etto, (4)<u>kondo</u> de ii desu ka.
Ten'in :	Hai, daijōbu desu.
	Dewa, kochira ni go-kinyū kudasai.
Jon :	(5)<u>Kono pen, karite</u> mo ii desu ka.
Ten'in :	Ee, ii desu yo.

---

❶
(1)	口座を開きたい _{こう ざ ひら}	kōza o hirakitai
(2)	パスポート	pasupōto
(3)	印鑑 _{いん かん}	inkan
(4)	サイン	sain
(5)	英語で _{えい ご}	Eigo de

---

❷
(1)	プールを利用したい _{り よう}	pūru o riyō shitai (riyō = use)
(2)	学生証 _{がく せい しょう}	gakusei-shō
(3)	水着とぼうし _{みず ぎ}	mizugi to bōshi (= swimsuit and cap)
(4)	これ	kore
(5)	ここに座って _{すわ}	koko ni suwatte

MEMO

～はお持ちですか。／ ... wa o-mochi desu ka. ／ Do you have ...? [polite expression]
_も

それから／sorekara／also, and

けっこうです。／Kekkō desu.／That's alright. → See p.118 "Kekkō desu"

Material

Check the words and situations of the three tasks below, then practice having a conversation using the left page.

Ex. Registering with a gym or rental store

会員になりたいんですが……。
かい いん

Kai-in ni naritai n desu ga....... / I'd like to become a member.

入会申し込み書
住 所
名 前
TEL

① Opening a bank account

口座を開きたいんですが……。
こう ざ   ひら

Kōza o hirakitai n desu ga....... / I'd like to open a bank account.

② Using a pool, gym, or other public facility

プールを利用したいんですが……。
り ょう

Pūru o riyō shitai n desu ga....... / I'd like to use the swimming pool.

You are often asked for:

1) 身分証明書 / mibun shōmei sho / ID
み ぶん しょう めい しょ

● 外国人登録証 / gaikoku-jin tōroku shō /
がい こく じん とう ろく しょう
alien registration card

● パスポート / pasupōto / passport

● 運転免許証 / unten menkyo shō / driver license
うん てん めん きょ しょう

● 学生証 / gakusei shō / student ID
がく せい しょう

● 健康保険証 / kenkō hokenshō /
けん こう ほ けん しょう
health insurance card

2) 住所がわかるもの / jūsho ga wakaru
じゅう しょ
mono / Proof of address

● 公共料金の請求書 /
こう きょうりょう きん   せい きゅう しょ
kōkyō-ryōkin no seikyū sho / Utility bills

3) その他 / sonota / Others
た

● 写真 / shashin / photo
しゃ しん

● 印鑑 / inkan / signature seal
いん かん

Listening

Listen to the conversation between the man and woman and choose the correct answer.

Q1 At a restaurant

1. The customer is not allowed to smoke because it is non-smoking area.
2. The customer wants to buy cigarettes.
3. The customer is not allowed to smoke because the waitress does not like cigarettes.

Q3 At a front desk

1. The woman said you cannot write in Roman letters.
2. The woman said you can write in Roman letters.
3. The woman would not let the man fill out an application.

Q2 At a drugstore

1. The man receives only a pamphlet.
2. The man can take either a pamphlet or a free sample.
3. The man receives both a pamphlet and a free sample.

Q4 In a taxi

1. The passenger paid with a 1,000-yen note.
2. The passenger paid with a 10,000-yen note.
3. The passenger paid with a credit card.

Role playing

Role play using the cards below.

1.

A: You go to a restaurant with good reviews, but it seems crowded. Ask if you can get a table without a reservation. If you are refused, take a business card or pamphlet placed near the cash register so you can make a reservation for another time.

B: You work at a restaurant. Right now there are no empty tables, so no one without a reservations may enter. Deny entry to anyone who does not have a reservation.

2.

A: You want to become a member at a gym. Tell this to the person behind the counter. Explain that you have no time to fill out forms today, and ask if you can take them home to fill out, bring back later, and if you may fill them out in English.

B: You work at a gym. A-san wants to become a member, so ask him/her to fill out the necessary paperwork. It is fine for A-san to take the forms home and bring them back later, and it is also okay if the forms are filled out in English.

Do you remember?

Use the phrases you have studied in this unit in situations ①–④ below.

①

②

③

④

Phrases for This Unit

Unit Phrases

- カードでいいですか。   Kādo de ii desu ka.   Can I pay by credit card?

- このペン、借りてもいい   Kono pen, karite mo ii   May I borrow this pen?
  ですか。   desu ka.

Useful expressions

- ～たいんですが……。   … tai n desu ga…….   I would like to.... / I want to....

- ～お持ちですか。   …o-mochi desu ka.   Do you have ...? [polite expression]

Check!

Now I can...

☐ Use simple sentences to ask for permission

☐ Confirm things to make sure documents are

submitted smoothly

Remember and Use!

● **Basic Verbs 8** ●

to eat たべる／taberu (→たべて／tabete)		to drink のむ／nomu (→のんで／nonde)	
to sit すわる／suwaru (→すわって／suwatte)		to enter はいる／hairu (→はいって／haitte)	
to write かく／kaku (→かいて／kaite)		to use つかう／tsukau (→つかって／tsukatte)	
to see, look, watch みる／miru (→みて／mite)		to copy コピーする／kopī suru (→コピーして／kopī shite)	

Learn the eight basic verbs above and use them with the phrase **"[verb-te]mo ii desu ka."**
～（て）もいいですか。／ [Verb-te] + mo ii desu ka. ／May/can I …?
→ See p.78 for more verbs

Japanese Verbs (dictionary form, masu-form and te-form)

Although Japanese verbs assume a variety of conjugations depending on tense and their function within a sentence, the three most basic verb forms are the **dictionary form, masu-form,** and **te-form**.

The **dictionary form,** also known as the **plain form,** frequently appears in casual conversation and is also used in different grammatical expressions. The **masu-form** appears in more polite conversation.

The **te-form**, which appears in Units 5 and 6, does not express tense, but can be conveniently used to create a wide array of grammatical expressions.

Verbs are divided into one of three groups depending on how they conjugate: **ru-verbs**, which have a simplistic conjugation, or **u-verbs**, ,which are the largest in number and the two **irregular verbs**.

See p.171, Grammar for more detailed explanations on verb conjugations and other issues.

● Verb Conjugation List ●

Ru-Verbs	Dictionary form		Masu-form		Te-form	
Eat	たべる	taberu	たべます	tabemasu	たべて	tabete
See, look	みる	miru	みます	mimasu	みて	mite
Open	あける	akeru	あけます	akemasu	あけて	akete

U-Verbs	Dictionary form		Masu-form		Te-form	
Use	つかう	tsukau	つかいます	tsukaimasu	つかって	tsukatte
Meet	あう	au	あいます	aimasu	あって	atte
Buy	かう	kau	かいます	kaimasu	かって	katte
Enter	はいる	hairu	はいります	hairimasu	はいって	haitte
Sit	すわる	suwaru	すわります	suwarimasu	すわって	suwatte
Go home	かえる	kaeru	かえります	kaerimasu	かえって	kaette
Drink	のむ	nomu	のみます	nomimasu	のんで	nonde
Read	よむ	yomu	よみます	yomimasu	よんで	yonde
Play, have fun	あそぶ	asobu	あそびます	asobimasu	あそんで	asonde
Write	かく	kaku	かきます	kakimasu	かいて	kaite

Irregular (2 verbs)	Dictionary form		Masu-form		Te-form	
Do	～する	-suru	～します	-shimasu	～して	-shite
- copy	コピー	kopī	コピー	kopī	コピー	kopī
- work	しごと	shigoto	しごと	shigoto	しごと	shigoto
- shop	かいもの	kaimono	かいもの	kaimono	かいもの	kaimono
Come	くる	kuru	きます	kimasu	きて	kite

Please wait a moment.

ちょっと待ってください。

Chotto matte kudasai.

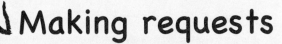

Making requests

依頼する

GOALS FOR UNIT 6

- Use simple sentences to make requests

- Invite someone to have something

- Give simple directions to a destination in a taxi

Phrase 1 — Making simple requests.

ちょっと待ってください。

ま

Chotto matte **kudasai.**

Please wait a moment.

Track
42

NOTE "**[Verb-te] kudasai**" is used to ask someone to please do something, and can be used to make a request or invite someone to do something.

Ex.

① ちょっと待ってください。

ま

② どうぞ食べてください。

た

① Chotto ma**tte kudasai**.

② **Dōzo** tabe**te kudasai**.

① Please wait a moment.

② Please help yourself.

A-1 [Verb-te]ください。

Make requests using the following words with the phrase "**[Verb-te] kudasai.**"

ちょっと待って ま chotto matte wait a moment	ちょっと来て き chotto kite come [here for a second]	それを見せて み sore o misete show me that	手伝って て つだ tetsudatte help

A-2 どうぞ[Verb-te]ください。

Invite someone to do something using the phrase "**Dōzo [Verb-te] kudasai.**"

食べて た tabete eat	飲んで の nonde drink	座って すわ suwatte sit
入って はい haitte enter	使って つか tsukatte use	見て み mite see, look, watch

What you can say with the phrase **"[Verb-te] kudasai."** in the following situations?
There may be more than one correct answer.

1. You are at a restaurant. You are not ready to order but the waiter has already come to your table.

2. The photocopy machine that you are using at a convenience store has a paper jam. Call one of the store clerks over.

3. You see a watch in a display case that you would like to take a closer look at. Ask the store clerk for help.

Put the words from Practice A-2 in < > and practice the conversation below.

① ·

田中　：ジョンさん、これ〈食べて〉もいいですか。
_{た なか}　　　　　　　　　　　　_た

ジョン：はい、どうぞ〈食べて〉ください。
　　　　　　　　　　　　_た

Tanaka : Jon-san, kore <tabete> mo ii desu ka.

Jon　　: Hai, dōzo <tabete> kudasai.

> Tanaka : John-san, can I eat this?
>
> John　　: Yes, please do.

② ·

ジョン：田中さん、ここ〈座って〉もいいですか。
　　　　_{た なか}　　　　_{すわ}

田中　：ええ、どうぞ〈座って〉ください。
_{た なか}　　　　　　　　_{すわ}

Jon　　: Tanaka-san, koko <suwatte> mo ii desu ka.

Tanaka : Ee, dōzo <suwatte> kudasai.

> John　　: Tanaka-san, can I sit here?
>
> Tanaka : Yes, by all means.

　　　　〜てもいいですか。／[verb-te] mo ii desu ka.／Can I / May I ...？→See p.70, Unit 5

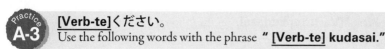

Practice A-3

[Verb-te]ください。
Use the following words with the phrase " **[Verb-te] kudasai.**"

- In a taxi -

角を左に曲がって かど ひだり ま kado o hidari ni magatte turn left at the corner	信号を右に曲がって しん ごう みぎ ま shingō o migi ni magatte turn right at the traffic light	（もうちょっと） まっすぐ行って い (mōchotto) massugu itte go straight (a little further)
そこで止めて と soko de tomete stop there	（明治）通りを行って めい じ どお い (Meiji)-dōri o itte go down Meiji street	その道をわたって みち sono michi o watatte cross the street

Practice B-3

Give directions to the taxi driver for where you want to go using the map on the right page.

Take a taxi to places (1) – (3) on the right page. Think about the example sentences and first ask the driver to take you to a nearby landmark. Once you arrive at the landmark, give directions to your final destination.

運転手 ：どちらまでですか。
うんてんしゅ

ジョン ：〈ニューホテル〉の近くまでお願いします。
ちか ねが

運転手 ：かしこまりました。
うんてんしゅ

– Near your destination –

運転手 ：このへんですか。
うんてんしゅ

ジョン ：もうちょっと〈まっすぐ行って〉ください。
い

あ、その〈ゲストハウス〉です。

そこで止めてください。
と

> Taxi driver : Where to?
> John : Take me to around the New Hotel, please.
> Taxi driver : Right away.
> - Near your destination -
> Taxi driver : Is this the area?
> John : Please <go straight a little>. Ah, that <guest house> is. Please stop there.

Untenshu : Dochira made desu ka.

Jon : <Nyū hoteru> no chikaku made onegaishimasu.

Untenshu : Kashikomarimashita.

– Near your destination –

Untenshu : Kono hen desu ka.

Jon : <Mō chotto massugu itte> kudasai.

A, sono <gesuto-hausu> desu.

Soko de tomete kudasai.

Map

Look at the map below and practice the conversation on the left page.

Ex. Destination: Gesuto-hausu / Guesthouse   Landmark: Nyū hoteru / The New Hotel

(1) Destination: (ILS) biru / The ILS Building   Landmark: Fuji byōin / Fuji Hospitall

(2) Destination: Apāto / Your apartment   Landmark: Sakura kōen / Sakura Park

(3) Destination: Sushi-ya / A sushi restaurant   Landmark: Sakura daigaku / Sakura University

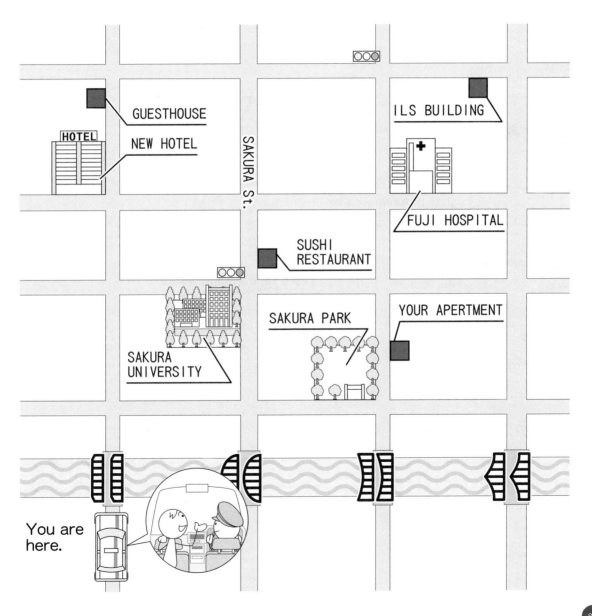

Phrase 2 — Use negative questions to make requests more polite.

ゆっくり話して**もらえませんか**。
はな

Yukkuri hanashite moraemasen ka.　　Could you speak more slowly?

Track 43

> **NOTE** "**[Verb-te] moraemasen ka**" is a polite way to make a request. (= "Could I have you …?") It uses the negative form of "**moraemasu**," which means "**to be able to receive**."

Ex.

ジョン ：すみません。もうちょっと<u>ゆっくり話して</u>もらえませんか。
　　　　　　　　　　　　　　　　　　　　　　はな

男の人 ：あ、すみません。わかりました。
おとこ ひと

Jon　　　　　　： Sumimasen. Mōchotto <u>yukkuri hanashite</u> **moraemasen ka.**

Otoko no hito : A, sumimasen. Wakarimashita.

> John　： I'm sorry, could you speak a little more slowly?
> Man　： Ah, I'm sorry about that. Yes.

Practice A

[Verb-te]もらえませんか。
Use the following words with the phrase " **[Verb-te] moraemasen ka.**"

ゆっくり話して はな yukkuri hanashite speak slowly	写真を撮って しゃ しん と shashin o totte take a picture	手伝って て つだ tetsudatte help me
この漢字を読んで かん じ よ kono kanji o yonde read this Kanji	地図を描いて ち ず か chizu o kaite draw a map	お金をくずして かね okane o kuzushite break a note
それを取って と sore o totte pass that to me	これを貸して か kore o kashite lend me this/let me use	荷物を預かって に もつ あず nimotsu o azukatte handle bags

84

B Ask for help from someone around you in the following situations.

1. You want to use a coin locker, but you don't have any coins.

2. You have a map with only Japanese written on it, and can't read the kanji for some of the place names, but want to know what they say.

3. After you check out of a hotel, you want to go to a few tourist attractions. Ask the hotel staff if they will look after your bags.

4. You are at a temple by yourself and want someone to take your picture.

5. You are at a convenience store and need to use the restroom.

> **Column**
>
> There are different levels of politeness when making requests in Japanese. After the most simplistic phrase, **[verb-te] + kudasai,** there are the affirmative and negative forms of **moraeru, [verb-te] moraemasu/moraemasen ka,** which are used in questions. These are followed by **itadakeru,** the *keigo*-form of **moraeru,** in expressions like **[verb-te] itadakemasu/itadakemasen ka,** which frequently appear in conversation. The politeness of a request can be modified simply by changing the words that come after the **te-form** of a verb. Use different request words depending on the situation and difficulty of a request.
>
> | | | |
> | --- | --- | --- |
> | | itadakemasen ka | |
> | | itadakemasu ka | |
> | **Verb te-form +** | moraemasen ka | Expressions with increasing politeness |
> | | moraemasu ka | |
> | | kudasai | |

Dialogue

Practice having a conversation by replacing the words in (1) – (3) with the words below.

-Tanaka-san is late to a party at an izakaya-

ジョン	:あ、田中さん。
	どうぞ (1)座ってください。
田中	:ありがとうございます。
ジョン	:どうぞ (2)飲んでください
田中	:あ、どうも。
ジョン	:おはし、取りましょうか。
田中	:あります。だいじょうぶです。
- Later -	
ジョン	:すみません、田中さん。
	(3)塩、取ってもらえませんか。
田中	:はい、どうぞ。

Jon	: A, Tanaka-san.
	Dōzo (1) suwatte kudasai.
Tanaka	: Arigatō gozaimasu.
Jon	: Dōzo (2) nonde kudasai.
Tanaka	: A, dōmo.
Jon	: O-hashi, torimashōka.
Tanaka	: Arimasu. Daijōbu desu.
Jon	: Sumimasen, Tanaka-san.
	(3) Shio, totte moraemasen ka.
Tanaka	: Hai, dōzo.

① (1) 入って   haitte
   (2) 食べて   tabete
   (3) しょうゆ   shōyu

② (1) こっちに来て   kocchi ni kite
   (2) この（お）皿、使って   kono (o)sara, tsukatte
   (3) さしみ   sashimi

MEMO

どうも。／Dōmo.／Thanks.

（お）はし、取りましょうか。／(O)hashi, torimashō ka.／Should I get you chopsticks?

塩／shio／salt

しょうゆ／shōyu／soy sauce

Listening

Listen to the conversation between the man and woman and choose the correct answer.

Q1 At the front desk of a hotel

1. The woman borrows an umbrella.
2. The woman lends an umbrella.
3. The woman buys an umbrella.

Q2 At an izakaya

1. The customer has already ordered some food.
2. The customer is not ready to leave the restaurant.
3. The customer is not ready to order.

Q3 In a taxi

1. The passenger asked the driver to turn left at a traffic light.
2. The passenger asked the driver to turn right.
3. The passenger asked the driver to go straight.

Q4 At a friend's house party

1. The man wants food.
2. The man wants an empty glass.
3. The man wants a clean plate.

Role playing

Role play using the cards below.

1.

> **A:** A Japanese friend has stopped by your house. After inviting your friend to come inside and sit down, offer him/her a cup of tea.

> **B:** You have come to A-san's house to give him/her a box of chocolate. Present the chocolate and suggest A-san eat it. If A-san offers you something, say thank you and accept it.

2.

> **A:** You are at an information center. Ask a staff member to show you a bus time table (=jikoku-hyō), and also ask them to make a copy of any pages you need.

> **B:** You work at an information center. Provide assistance with A-san's requests.

Do you remember?

Use the phrases you have studied in this unit in situations ①–③ below.

Could you …?

Please ….

Could you …?

Phrases for This Unit

Unit Phrases

● ちょっと待ってください。   Chotto matte kudasai.   Please wait a moment.

● ゆっくり話して   Yukkuri hanashite   Could you speak more slowly?
もらえませんか。   moraemasen ka.

Useful expressions

● どうぞ、食べてください。   Dōzo tabete kudasai.   Please help yourself

● どうも   Dōmo   thanks

● ～までお願いします。   ... made onegaishimasu.   Please take me to ... .
[used when giving
directions to a taxi driver]

Check!

Now I can...

☐ Use simple sentences to make a request

☐ Invite someone to have something

☐ Give simple directions to a destination in a taxi

Customer Service

When buying a present for someone at a Japanese shop, several stores will provide free giftwrapping upon request. However, boxes and special wrapping may come at a fee, so be sure to confirm this beforehand.

Stores will also give multiple bags for multiple items at the customer's request. Department stores, large grocery stores, and stores that sell furniture and electronics typically provide home delivery. The cost of delivery depends on the distance traveled, with nearby places sometimes being free, so be sure to confirm before making any arrangements.

● Helpful Phrases

1. Requesting giftwrapping

(1) すみません、ラッピングしてもらえますか。

> Sumimasen, rappingu shite moraemasu ka.
> Excuse me, would you giftwrap this for me?

(2) 無料ですか。有料ですか。

> Muryō desu ka. Yūryō desu ka. *
> Is wrapping here free or does it cost something?
> *muryō: free / yūryō: paid

2. Arranging delivery

(1) すみません、これ、配達してもらえませんか。

> Sumimasen, kore, haitatsu shite moraemasen ka.
> Excuse me, could I have this delivered?

(2) 〜まで、いくらかかりますか。

> ... made ikura kakarimasu ka?
> How much does it cost [to have it delivered] to ...?

What you must provide

住所／jūsho／address

名前／namae／name

電話番号／denwa bangō／phone number

配達日時／haitatsu-nichiji／delivery date and time

Does this (train) go to Yokohama?

これ、横浜に行きますか。

よこ はま

Kore, Yokohama ni ikimasu ka.

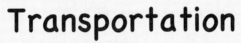

Transportation

交通

GOALS FOR UNIT 7

- Confirm how to get to a place with public transportation

- Ask for the best route somewhere with public transportation

- Ask about the time and cost required to reach a destination

これ、横浜に行きますか。
よこはま

Kore, Yokohama ni ikimasu ka.   Does this (train) go to Yokohama ?

Track
49

NOTE   **"Ikimasu"** means **"to go."** The phrase **"Kore, [place] ni ikimasu ka?"** is used to ask if a nearby mode of transportation goes to a specific destination.

Ex.

ジョン ：すみません。**これ、横浜に行きますか。**
よこはま

駅員 　：ええ、行きますよ。
えきいん　　　　　い

Jon   : Sumimasen. **Kore,** <u>Yokohama</u> **ni ikimasu ka.**
Eki-in : Ee, ikimasuyo.

John   : Excuse me. Does this (train) go to Yokohama?
Station staff : Yes, it does.

Practice
A-1

これ、＿＿＿＿に行きますか。
　　　　　　　　い

Use the following words with the phrase **"Kore, ＿＿＿ ni ikimasu ka."**

横浜 よこ はま Yokohama Yokohama	東京 とう きょう Tōkyō Tokyo	新大阪 しん おお さか Shin-Ōsaka Shin-Osaka	成田空港 なり た くう こう Narita kūkō Narita Airport

A-2

[Place]は、＿＿＿＿ですよ。

Answer the questions from Practice A-1 using the phrase **"[Place] wa ＿＿＿ desu yo."**

2番線 に ばん せん ni-ban sen Platform 2	ちがうホーム chigau hōmu a different platform	ちがう線 せん chigau sen a different train line
次の電車 つぎ でん しゃ tsugi no densha the next train	あっち acchi over there	反対 はん たい hantai the opposite side

B Put the words from Practice A-1 or A-2 in < > and practice the conversation below.

- A train is stopped at the platform -

ジョン ：すみません、これ、^{A-1}〈横浜〉に行きますか。
　　　　　　　　　　　　よこはま

駅員　：はい、行きますよ。／いいえ、^{A-1}〈横浜〉は^{A-2}〈2番線〉ですよ。
えきいん　　　い　　　　　　　　　　よこはま　　　　に ばんせん

ジョン ：ありがとうございます。

Jon　　　: Sumimasen, kore, ^{A-1}<Yokohama > ni
　　　　　　ikimasu ka.

Eki-in　: Hai, ikimasu yo.
　　　　　 / Iie, ^{A-1}<Yokohama> wa ^{A-2}< ni-ban sen >
　　　　　　desu yo.

Jon　　　: Arigatō gozaimasu.

John	: Excuse me, does this (train) go to Yokohama?
Station staff	: Yes, it does. / No, (the train for) Yokohama (stops at) Platform 2.
John	: Thank you.

Phrase 2 Confirm how to get to a destination.

新宿までどうやって行けばいいですか。
しんじゅく　　　　　　　　　　い

Shinjuku made dōyatte ikeba ii desu ka.

Track 50

How do I get to Shinjuku?

NOTE "**Made**" and "**dōyatte**" mean "**to**" and "**how**", respectively. The phrase "**Dōyatte ikeba ii desu ka.**" is used when asking directions to a destination.

Ex.

ジョン ：新宿までどうやって行けばいいですか。
　　　　しんじゅく　　　　　　　　い
駅員 ：総武線で一本ですよ。
えきいん　そうぶせん　いっぽん

Jon	: <u>Shinjuku</u> **made dōyatte ikeba ii desu ka**.
Eki-in	: Sōbu-sen de ippon desu yo.

John	: How do I get to Shinjuku?
Station staff	: You can go straight there with the Sobu-Line.

 Practice A

＿＿＿＿までどうやって行けばいいですか。
　　　　　　　　　い

Use the following words with the phrase " ＿＿**made dōyatte ikeba ii desu ka.**"

新宿
しんじゅく
Shinjuku
Shinjuku

渋谷
しぶや
Shibuya
Shibuya

東京
とうきょう
Tōkyō
Tokyo

秋葉原
あきはばら
Akihabara
Akihabara

IKEBUKURO

UENO

SHINJUKU   IIDABASHI   AKIHABARA

YOTSUYA   OCHANOMIZU   KANDA

YOYOGI

SHIBUYA   TŌKYŌ

MEGURO

CHŪO-SEN
SŌBU-SEN
YAMANOTE-SEN

Ask how to get to the places listed in Practice A using the map on page 94 and following the pattern in (1) or (2) below.

- Currently at Yoyogi -

ジョン ：すみません。^{A-1}〈東京〉まで、どうやって行けばいいですか。

駅員 ：(1)〈山手線〉で一本ですよ。

(2)〈総武線〉に乗って、〈四谷〉で〈中央線〉に乗りかえですよ。

ジョン ：ありがとうございます。

Jon	: Sumimasen. ^{A-1} < Tōkyō > made dōyatte ikeba ii desu ka.
Eki-in	: (1) < Yamanote-sen > de ippon desu yo. (2) < Sōbu-sen > ni notte, < Yotsuya > de < Chūō-sen > ni norikae desu yo.
Jon	: Arigatō gozaimasu.

John	: Excuse me. How do I get to Tokyo?
Station staff	: (1) You can go straight there with the Yamanote-Line. (2) You can take the Sobu-Line and transfer to the Chuo-Line at Yotsuya.
John	: Thank you.

MEMO

(〜線で) 一本／(...sen de) ippon／directly on the ... line

〜に乗って／... ni notte／get on ... [the te-form is used in conjunction with other verbs]

(Aで) B線に乗りかえです。／(A de) B-sen ni norikae desu.／Transfer to B-line (at A).

Phrase 3　Ask how much time it takes to get somewhere.

東京から京都までどのぐらいかかりますか。
とうきょう　　きょうと

Track
51

Tōkyō kara Kyōto **made donogurai kakarimasu ka.**

How long does it take from Tokyo **to** Kyoto?

NOTE　**"A kara B made"** means **"from A to B"**, the word **"donogurai"** means **"how long?"** and **"kakarimasu"** means **"take"** when referring to time. The phrase **"Donogurai kakarimasu ka?"** is used when asking how much time it takes to get somewhere.

Ex.

ジョン　：東京から京都までどのぐらいかかりますか。
　　　　　とうきょう　　きょうと

田中　：新幹線で2時間半ぐらいですよ。
たなか　　しんかんせん　　じかんはん

Jon　　　：Tōkyō kara <u>Kyōto</u> **made donogurai kakarimasu ka.**

Tanaka　：Shinkansen de 2-jikan han gurai desu yo.

John　　：How long does it take from Tokyo to Kyoto?

Tanaka　：It's about two and a half hours by Shinkansen.

Practice
A

_____ までどのぐらいかかりますか。
Use the following words with the phrase "_____ **made donogurai kakarimasu ka."**

① 築地 つきじ Tsukiji Tsukiji	② 東京タワー とうきょう Tōkyō tawā Tokyo Tower
③ 箱根 はこね Hakone Hakone	④ 日光 にっこう Nikkō Nikko

Practice B Look up how to say lengths of time (p. 103) and answer the questions in Practice A using the information below.

①	地下鉄 ちかてつ chikatetsu subway	➡	15分 ふん 15-fun 15 minutes	②	歩いて* ある aruite on foot	➡	20分 ぷん 20-pun 20 minutes
③	電車 でんしゃ densha train	➡	1時間半 じ かん はん 1-jikan han 1.5 hours	④	車 くるま kuruma car	➡	2時間半 じ かん はん 2-jikan han 2.5 hours

＊ When describing how long it takes to walk somewhere, the verb **"aruite"** is used without particles (compare **"densha de"** with **"aruite"**.)

ジョン ：ここから〈築地〉までどのぐらいかかりますか。
　　　　　　　　　つき じ
田中　：〈地下鉄〉で、(たぶん)〈15分〉ぐらいです。
た なか　　　ち か てつ　　　　　　　　　　ふん
ジョン ：そうですか。

Jon	: Koko kara < Tsukiji > made donogurai kakarimasu ka.
Tanaka	: < Chikatetsu > de (tabun) < 15-fun > gurai desu.
Jon	: Sō desu ka.

John	: How long does it take to get from here to Tsukiji?
Tanaka	: On the subway, (probably) about 15 minutes.
John	: Okay.

MEMO

〜ぐらいです。／ ... gurai desu. ／ It's about....

たぶん／ tabun ／ probably/I think

Look at the table on the right page and practice the conversation pattern below.

ジョン	：鈴木さん、東京から(1)京都まで どうやって行けばいいですか。	Jon	: Suzuki-san, Tōkyo kara (1) <u>Kyōto</u> made dōyatte ikeba ii desu ka.
鈴木	：うーん、(2)バスか(3)新幹線ですね。	Suzuki	: Ūn, (2) <u>basu</u> ka (3) <u>shinkansen</u> desu ne.
ジョン	：(2)バスでどのぐらいかかりますか。	Jon	: (2) <u>Basu</u> de donogurai kakarimasu ka.
鈴木	：たぶん(4)6時間ぐらいです。	Suzuki	: Tabun (4) <u>6-jikan</u> gurai desu.
ジョン	：いくらぐらいかかりますか。	Jon	: Ikura gurai kakarimasu ka.
鈴木	：そうですね……。 (5)7000円ぐらいだと思いますよ。	Suzuki	: Sō desu ne...... . (5) <u>7000-en</u> gurai da to omoimasu yo.
ジョン	：そうですか。ありがとうございます。	Jon	: Sō desu ka. Arigatō gozaimasu.

①
(1) 富士山　　　　　　Fuji-san
(2) バス　　　　　　　basu
(3) 車　　　　　　　　kuruma
(4) 2時間半　　　　　2-jikan-han
(5) 1500円　　　　　 1500-en

②
(1) 沖縄　　　　　　　Okinawa
(2) 船　　　　　　　　fune
(3) 飛行機　　　　　　hikōki
(4) 3日間　　　　　　mikka-kan
(5) 20000円　　　　　20000-en

MEMO

いくらぐらいかかりますか。／Ikura gurai kakarimasu ka.／About how much does it cost?

～（だ）と思います。／...(da) to omoimasu.／I think that ....

船／fune／ship / boat

飛行機／hikōki／airplane

Material

Use the picture below to practice having a conversation.

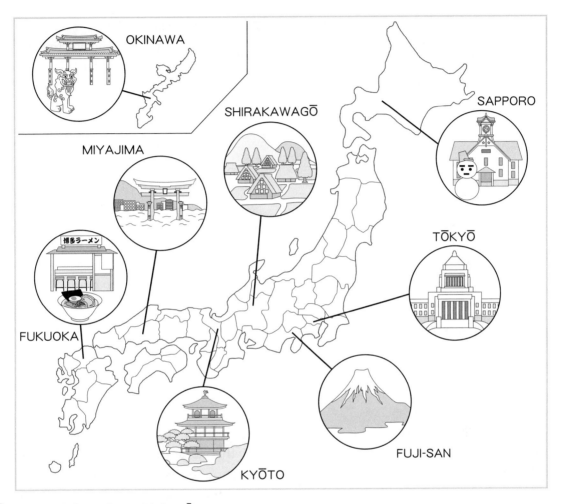

OKINAWA

SHIRAKAWAGŌ

SAPPORO

MIYAJIMA

TŌKYŌ

FUKUOKA

FUJI-SAN

KYŌTO

【Time and Cost from Tokyo】

京都 Kyōto		富士山 Fuji-san		沖縄 Okinawa		福岡 Fukuoka	
Bus	Shinkansen	Bus	Car	Airplane	Ship	Airplane	Shinkansen
6 hours	2.5 hours	2 hours	2 hours	2.5 hours	3 days	2 hours	5 hours
7000 yen	20000 yen	1500 yen	3000 yen	30000 yen	20000 yen	20000 yen	25000 yen

Listening

Listen to the conversation between the man and woman and choose the correct answer.

Q1 On a station platform, pointing at a train

1. The train currently at the platform goes to Hakone.
2. The next train goes to Hakone.
3. A train at a different platform goes to Hakone.

Q3 On a street

1. It takes about 10 minutes from here to Tokyo Dome by bus.
2. It takes about 10 minutes from here to Tokyo Dome by bicycle.
3. It takes about 10 minutes from here to Tokyo Dome by train.

Q2 At a train station ticket counter

1. The subway goes straight to Roppongi Hills.
2. The bus goes straight to Roppongi Hills.
3. It takes a bus and a subway ride to get to Roppongi Hills.

Q4 Talking with a co-worker at work

1. It takes about 3 hours from Tokyo to Osaka by plane.
2. It takes about 3 hours from Tokyo to Osaka by Shinkansen.
3. It takes about 1 hour from Tokyo to Osaka by Shinkansen.

Role playing

Role play using the cards below.

1.

A: You are currently in Shibuya but want to go to Iidabashi. Ask a person nearby how to get there and how long it takes.

B: You are currently in Shibuya. Look at the picture on page 94 and answer A-san's questions. When there is something you don't know, simply say you don't know.

2.

A: You want to go to B-san's hometown. Ask B-san how to get there, how long it takes, and how much it costs.

B: A-san wants to go to your hometown. Answer his or her questions.

Do you remember?

Use the phrases you have studied in this unit in situations ①–③ below.

①

How long ···
to Tokyo?

20 mins.

②

How to
get to
Tokyo?

Chūō Line.

③

To Tokyo?

Opposite
side.

Phrases for This Unit

Unit Phrases

● これ、横浜に行きますか。
よこはま

Kore, Yokohama ni ikimasu ka.

Does this [train] go to Yokohama?

● 新宿までどうやっていけば
しんじゅく
いいですか。

Shinjuku made dō yatte ikeba ii desu ka.

How do you get to Shinjuku?

● 東京から京都までどのぐらい
とうきょう   きょうと
かかりますか。

Tōkyō kara Kyōto made dono gurai kakarimasu ka.

How long does it take from Tokyo to Kyoto?

Useful expressions

● ～ぐらいです。

… gurai desu.

It's about ….

● たぶん

tabun

probably/I think

● いくらぐらいかかりますか。

Ikura gurai kakarimasu ka.

About how much does it cost?

● ～（だ）と思います。
おも

… (da) to omoimasu.

I think that ….

Check!

Now I can...

☐ Confirm how to get to a place with public transportation

☐ Ask for the best route somewhere with public transportation

☐ Ask about the time and cost required to reach a destination

Remember and Use!

● TIME and HOURS

TIME −時(−じ −ji)		MINUTES −分(−ふん -fun / −ぷん -pun)			
-AM / -PM 午前(ごぜん gozen)／午後(ごご gogo)		5	ごふん go-**fun**	10	じゅっぷん ju**ppun**
		15	じゅうごふん jūgo-**fun**	20	にじゅっぷん niju**ppun**
		25	にじゅうごふん nijūgo-**fun**	30	さんじゅっぷん／はん sanju**ppun** / han
		35	さんじゅうごふん sanjūgo-**fun**	40	よんじゅっぷん yonju**ppun**
		45	よんじゅうごふん yonjūgo-**fun**	50	ごじゅっぷん goju**ppun**
what time = 何時(なんじ nan-ji)		55	ごじゅうごふん gojūgo-**fun**	?	なんぷん nam**pun**

Clock face labels: じゅういちじ jūichi-ji, じゅうにじ jūni-ji, いちじ ichi-ji, じゅうじ jū-ji, にじ ni-ji, くじ ku-ji, さんじ san-ji, はちじ hachi-ji, よじ yo-ji, しちじ shichi-ji, ろくじ roku-ji, ごじ go-ji

→ See p.177, Grammar

1. Fill out the Q&A like the example below.

(1) Q: 今、何時ですか。　　　　　　　　　　Ima nan-ji desu ka.

　　A: (ごぜん)ごじじゅっぷんです。　　　(Gozen) go-ji juppun desu.

　　Ex. 5:10 a.m.　　1. 7:40 a.m.　　2. 9:15 p.m.　　3. 8:50 a.m.　　4. 4:05 p.m.　　5. 1:30 p.m.

(2) Q: 仕事は何時からですか。　　　　　Shigoto wa nan-ji kara desu ka.

　　A: (ごぜん)はちじはんからです。　　(Gozen) hachi-ji han kara desu.

　　Ex. 仕事 shigoto 8:30 a.m.　　1. 授業 jugyō 9:50 a.m.　　2. 店 mise 10:00 a.m.

HOURS 時間(じかん −jikan)	MINUTES 分(ふん -fun / ぷん -pun)
Ex. 2 hours → にじかん　　ni-jikan 4.5 hours → よじかんはん　　yo-jikan han	Same as the readings for minutes in a timetable. Note: 3 hours and 20 minutes → さんじかんにじゅっぷん　san-jikan nijuppun

2. Fill out the Q&A like the example below.

(1) Q: どのぐらいかかりますか。　　　　Donogurai kakarimasu ka.

　　A: にじかんぐらいです。　　　　　Ni-jikan gurai desu.

　　Ex. 2 hours　　1. 1 hour　　2. 2 hours 15 minutes　　3. 4 hours 45 minutes　　4. 9.5 hours

● CALENDAR

DATES −日（−にち −nichi / −か −ka）						+＿に / ＿ni [particle]
1 ついたち **tsuitachi**	**2** ふつか **futsuka**	**3** みっか **mikka**	**4** よっか **yokka**	**5** いつか **itsuka**	**6** むいか **muika**	**7** なのか **nanoka**
8 ようか **yōka**	**9** ここのか **kokonoka**	**10** とおか **tōka**	11 じゅういちにち jūichi-nichi	12 じゅうににち jūni-nichi	13 じゅうさんにち jūsan-nichi	**14** じゅうよっか **jūyokka**
15 じゅうごにち jūgo-nichi	16 じゅうろくにち jūroku-nichi	17 じゅうしちにち jūshichi-nichi	18 じゅうはちにち jūhachi-nichi	19 じゅうくにち jūku-nichi	**20** はつか **hatsuka**	21 にじゅういちにち nijūichi-nichi
22 にじゅうににち nijūni-nichi	23 にじゅうさんにち nijūsan-nichi	**24** にじゅうよっか **nijūyokka**	25 にじゅうごにち nijūgo-nichi	26 にじゅうろくにち nijūroku-nichi	27 にじゅうしちにち nijūshichi-nichi	28 にじゅうはちにち nijūhachi-nichi
29 にじゅうくにち nijūku-nichi	30 さんじゅうにち sanjū-nichi	31 さんじゅういちにち sanjūichi-nichi	* Exceptional readings are in **bold**			

MONTH −月（−がつ −gatsu）					+＿に / ＿ni [particle]
1 January いちがつ ichi-gatsu	2 February にがつ ni-gatsu	3 March さんがつ san-gatsu	4 April しがつ shi-gatsu	5 May ごがつ go-gatsu	6 June ろくがつ roku-gatsu
7 July しちがつ shichi-gatsu	8 August はちがつ hachi-gatsu	9 September くがつ ku-gatsu	10 October じゅうがつ jū-gatsu	11 November じゅういちがつ jūichi-gatsu	12 December じゅうにがつ jūni-gatsu

VOCABURALY				+~~に~~ / ~~ni~~	DURATION OF THE TIME		
	Last	This	Next			1	2
Year	きょねん kyonen	ことし kotoshi	らいねん rainen	Year	＋ねん（かん） +nen(kan)	いちねん（かん） ichi-nen(kan)	にねん（かん） ni-nen(kan)
Month	せんげつ sengetsu	こんげつ kongetsu	らいげつ raigetsu	Month	＋かげつ（かん） +kagetsu(kan)	いっかげつ ikkagetsu(kan)	にかげつ ni-kagetsu(kan)
Week	せんしゅう senshū	こんしゅう konshū	らいしゅう raishū	Week	＋しゅうかん +shūkan	いっしゅうかん isshūkan	にしゅうかん ni-shūkan
Day	きのう kinō	きょう kyō	あした ashita	Day	[Date]（＋かん） [Date](+kan)	いちにち* ichi-nichi	ふつか（かん） futsuka(kan)

＊ Note the difference between "ichi-nichi" (one day) and "tsuitachi" (the 1st day of the month)

I'm going to an art museum.

美術館に行きます。
び じゅつ かん い
Bijutsukan ni ikimasu.

Talking about plans and activities

予定や行動について話す

GOALS FOR UNIT 8

- Talk about plans and what you are about to do

- Ask about things that have happened and places people have been to

- Talk about interests and wants

Phrase 1

Talk about what you are about to do.

美術館に行きます。
びじゅつかん　い

Bijutsukan **ni ikimasu.**

Track 57

I'm going to an art museum.

NOTE "[Place] ni ikimasu" means "[I am] going to go to [place]". The phrase " ___ ni ikimasu" can be combined with verb stems to indicate a purpose for going, as in "<u>tabe</u> ni ikimasu" (= "I am going to <u>eat</u>.")

Ex.

田中　：どこに行きますか。
たなか　　　　　　い

ジョン：美術館に行きます。
　　　　びじゅつかん　い

Tanaka : Doko ni ikimasu ka.

Jon　　 : <u>Bijutsukan</u> **ni ikimasu.**

Tanaka : Where are you going?

John　　 : I'm going to an art museum.

Practice A

_____に行きます。
　　　　い

Use the following words with the phrase " _____ ni ikimasu."

美術館 びじゅつかん bijutsukan art museum	新宿 しんじゅく Shinjuku Shinjuku	友だちのうち とも tomodachi no uchi a friend's house
本屋 ほんや hon-ya bookstore → *See Appendix, Shops*	買い物 か もの kaimono shopping	公園 こうえん kōen park
飲み の nomi ... to drink	ごはんを食べ た gohan o tabe ... to have food	うちに帰ります* かえ uchi ni kaerimasu* go home

* "Kaerimasu" is used instead of "ikimasu" when one is going to one's own house.

B Put the words from Practice A in < > and practice having a conversation.

John-san runs into his co-worker Tanaka-san on the way home from work.

ジョン ：おつかれさまです。

田中 ：おつかれさまです。ジョンさん、これからどこに行きますか。

ジョン ：〈新宿〉に行きます。田中さんは？

田中 ：私はうちに帰ります。

ジョン ：じゃ、駅まで一緒に行きましょう。

田中 ：はい、行きましょう。

Jon : Otsukaresama desu.

Tanaka : Otsukaresama desu. Jon-san, korekara doko ni ikimasu ka.

Jon : < Shinjuku > ni ikimasu. Tanaka-san wa?

Tanaka : Watashi wa uchi ni kaerimasu.

Jon : Ja, eki made issho ni ikimashō.

Tanaka : Hai, ikimashō.

John : Hello.

Tanaka : Hello. John-san, where are you going rignt now?

John : I'm going to Shinjuku. How about you, Tanaka-san?

Tanaka : I'm going home.

John : Well, then let's go to the station together.

Tanaka : Okay, let's do that.

MEMO

おつかれさまです。／Otsukaresama desu.／Hello. / Goodbye. ["Otsukaresama desu" is a greeting used in the workplace instead of "Hello." or "Goodbye."]

これから／korekara／right now, from now

駅まで／eki made／[up] to the station

一緒に／issho ni／together

行きましょう。／Ikimashō.／Let's go.

Phrase 2　Talk about prior actions.

昨日はうちで日本語を勉強し**ました**。
きのう　　　　　　　にほんご　　べんきょう

Kinō wa uchi de Nihon-go o benkyō shimashita.

Track
58

I studied Japanese at home yesterday.

NOTE　In the past tense, masu verbs end in **"-mashita"**. The particle **"de"** is used to indicate the place where an action occurred. **"Nani o shimashita ka"** means **"What did you do?"**

Ex.

田中　：昨日は何をしましたか。
たなか　きのう　なに

ジョン　：(昨日は)うちで日本語を勉強し**ました**。
　　　　　きのう　　　　にほんご　　べんきょう

Tanaka　: Kinō wa nani o shimashita ka.

Jon　　 : (Kinō wa) uchi de Nihon-go o
　　　　　 benkyō shi**mashita.**

Tanaka : What did you do yesterday?

John　　: I studied Japanese at home
　　　　　 (yesterday).

Practice A-1

_____ました。

Change the **"masu"** portion of the follwing words to **"_____ mashita."**

日本語を勉強し(ます)	友だちに会い(ます)	ごはんを食べ(ます)
にほんご　べんきょう	とも　あ	た
Nihon-go o benkyō shi(masu)	tomodachi ni ai(masu)	gohan o tabe(masu)
study Japanese	meet a friend	have some food

本を読み(ます)	テレビを見(ます)	散歩し(ます)
ほん　よ	み	さんぽ
hon o yomi(masu)	terebi o mi(masu)	sampo shi(masu)
read a book	watch TV	take a walk

買い物し(ます)	仕事し(ます)	うちにい(ます)
か　もの	しごと	
kaimono shi(masu)	shigoto shi(masu)	uchi ni i(masu)
go shopping	work	stay at home

Practice **A-2**

_____は、何をしましたか。
Use the following words with the phrase "_____ **wa nani o shimashita ka.**"

昨日 きのう kinō yesterday	週末 しゅうまつ shūmatsu weekend	先週 せん しゅう senshū last week → *See p.104, Calendar*

Practice **B**

Put the words from Practice A-1 and A-2 in < > below and the name of a place in _____ practice
having a conversation.

田中
たなか ：ジョンさん、^{A-2}〈昨日〉はどこか行きましたか。
　　　　　　　　　　　きのう

ジョン ：新宿に行きました。／うちにいました。
　　　　しんじゅく

田中
たなか ：新宿／うちで何をしましたか。
　　　　しんじゅく

ジョン ：^{A-1}〈日本語を勉強し〉ました。それから、^{A-1}〈ごはんを食べ〉ました。
　　　　　　にほんご　　べんきょう　　　　　　　　　　　　　　　た

　　　　田中さんは、^{A-2}〈昨日〉何をしましたか。
　　　　たなか　　　　　　　きのう　なに

田中
たなか ：私はうちで^{A-1}〈本を読み〉ました。
　　　　　　　　　　　　ほん　よ

Tanaka : Jon-san, ^{A-2}< kinō > wa dokoka ikimashita ka.
Jon　　 : <u>Shinjuku</u> ni ikimashita. / Uchi ni imashita.
Tanaka : <u>Shinjuku / uchi</u> de nani o shimashita ka.
Jon　　 : ^{A-1}< Nihon-go o benkyō shi > mashita.
　　　　　Sorekara, ^{A-1}<gohan o tabe> mashita.
　　　　　Tanaka-san wa ^{A-2}< kinō > nani o shimashita ka.
Tanaka : Watashi wa <u>uchi</u> de ^{A-1}<hon o yomi> mashita.

Tanaka : John-san, did you go anywhere
　　　　　yesterday?
John　　 : I went to Shinjuku. / I stayed at
　　　　　home.
Tanaka : What did you do at Shinjuku /
　　　　　home?
John　　 : I studied Japanese. Then, I had
　　　　　something to eat.
　　　　　What did you do yesterday,
　　　　　Tanaka-san?
Tanaka : I read a book at home.

MEMO

どこか行きましたか。／Dokoka ikimashita ka.／Did you go somewhere/anywhere?
　　　い

それから／sorekara／and, after that

[Place]で[Verb]／[Place] de [Verb]／[Verb] at [place] *denotes the location of an action

109

Phrase 3　Talk about what you want to do.

すもうを見_みたいです。

Sumō o mitai desu.

I want to watch sumo wrestling.

Track
59

NOTE The verb-ending "_____**tai desu**" attaches to verb stems to mean "**I want to/would like to [verb]**". For example, "**tabemasu**" → "**tabetai desu**" (I want to eat.)

Ex.

田中_{たなか}：今度_{こんど}の休_{やす}み、何_{なに}をしますか。

ジョン：すもうを見_みたいです。

Tanaka : Kondo no yasumi, nani o shimasu ka.

Jon　　: Sumō o mi**tai desu**.

Tanaka : What are you going to do next holiday?

John　　: I want to watch sumo wrestling.

Practice A-1

_____たいです。

Change the "**masu**" portion of the follwing words to " _____ **tai desu**."

すもうを見_み（ます） sumō o mi(masu) watch sumo wrestling	服_{ふく}を買_かい（ます） fuku o kai(masu) buy clothes	日本語_{にほんご}を勉強_{べんきょう}し（ます） Nihon-go o benkyō shi(masu) study Japanese
遊_{あそ}びに行_いき（ます） asobi ni iki(masu) go hang out (with friends)	旅行_{りょこう}に行_いき（ます） ryokō ni iki(masu) go on a trip	海_{うみ}／山_{やま}に行_いき（ます） umi/ yama ni iki(masu) go to the beach / mountains
家族_{かぞく}に会_あい（ます） kazoku ni ai(masu) see (my) family	ジョギングし（ます） jogingu shi(masu) jog	ゆっくりし（ます） yukkuri shi(masu) relax/take it easy

、何をしますか。

Use the following words with the phrase " [Time period], **nani o shimasu ka.**"

今度の休み こんど やす kondo no yasumi the next holiday/day off	週末 しゅうまつ shūmatsu weekend	ゴールデンウィーク gōruden wīku Golden Week*	夏休み なつ やす natsu-yasumi summer break

＊ Golden week is a series of week-long holidays that occurs from late April to early May.

 Put the words from Practice A-1 and A-2 in < > and practice having a conversation.

田中 ：ジョンさん、^{A-2}〈今度の休み〉、何をしますか。
たなか

ジョン ：^{A-1}〈すもうを見〉たいです。田中さんは？
み たなか

田中 ：私も^{A-1}〈すもうを見〉たいです。／私は^{A-1}〈ゆっくりし〉たいです。
たなか み

Tanaka : Jon-san, ^{A-2}< konodo no yasumi >,
nani o shimasu ka.

Jon : ^{A-1}< Sumō o mi > tai desu.

Tanaka-san wa?

Tanaka : Watashi mo ^{A-1}< sumō o mi > tai desu.
/ Watashi wa ^{A-1}<yukkuri shi> tai desu.

> Tanaka : John-san, what are you doing on your
> next day off?
>
> John : I want to see some sumo. How about
> you?
>
> Tanaka : I want to see sumo wrestling, too. /
> I want to relax.

Column

The English language uses the phrase "Would you like …?" to make recommendations or invite a person to do something, but the Japanese when making invitations phrase **"…tai desu ka."** is not used in Japanese.

For example, the phrase "Would you like a coffee?" translates into Japanese as **"Kōhī o nomimasu ka."** or **"Kōhī o nomimasen ka."**, or literally **"Will you/Won't you have coffee?"**

Ending these sorts of question with **"masu ka"** asks the listener for his or her intent, while **"masen ka"** is more of an invitation.

Practice having a conversation by replacing the words in (1)—(4) with the words below.

田中 たなか	：ジョンさん、週末、何をしましたか。 　　しゅうまつ　なに
ジョン	：(1)新宿でごはんを食べました。 　　しんじゅく　　　　　た 　　田中さんは？ 　　たなか
田中 たなか	：私はうちでゆっくりしました。 　　わたし 　　今度の週末は何をしますか。 　　こんど　しゅうまつ　なに
ジョン	：(2)こどもと(3)公園に行きます。 　　　　　　　　　こうえん　い
田中 たなか	：そうですか。(3)公園で何をします 　　　　　　　　こうえん　なに 　　か。
ジョン	：(4)写真を撮りたいです。 　　　しゃしん　と
田中 たなか	：いいですね。

Tanaka	: Jon-san, shūmatsu nani o shimashita ka.
Jon	: (1)Shinjuku de gohan o tabemashita. Tanaka san wa?
Tanaka	: Watashi wa uchi de yukkuri shimashita. Kondo no shūmatsu wa nani o shimasuka.
Jon	: (2)Kodomo to (3)kōen ni ikimasu.
Tanaka	: Sō desu ka. (3)Kōen de nani o shimasuka.
Jon	: (4)Shashin o toritai desu.
Tanaka	: Ii desu ne.

①
(1) サイクリングしました　　saikuringu shimashita
(2) 友だち　　tomodachi
　　とも
(3) 海　　umi
　　うみ
(4) 本を読みたい　　hon o yomitai
　　ほん　よ

②
(1) 友だちに会いました。　　tomodachi ni aimashita
　　とも　あ
(2) 家族　　kazoku
　　かぞく
(3) ショッピングモール　　shoppingu-mōru (=shopping mall)
(4) おみやげを買いたい　　omiyage o kaitai (omiyage=souvenir)
　　　　　　か

> **MEMO**
>
> [Person] と [verb] ／ [Person] to [verb] ／ [verb] with a [person]
>
> To say "by myself" or "alone", use the phrase "hidori de".

Listening

Listen to the conversation between the man and woman and choose the correct answer.

Q1 After work

1. The woman is going to a drug store.
2. The man is going to buy food with a friend.
3. The woman is going to a bookstore.

Q3 Two friends are talking about the summer break

1. They are going to the beach together.
2. The man doesn't want to go to the beach.
3. The woman wants to relax at home.

Q2 Monday morning at work

1. The woman went to a park with her family.
2. The man is going to work on the weekend.
3. The man and woman went to a park.

Q4 Two friends are talking

1. The man wants to study Japanese on the weekend.
2. The man wants to go out somewhere.
3. The man wants to study with the woman.

Role playing

Role play using the cards below.

1.

A: You are showing B-san around Tokyo. Ask B-san questions like where he/she wants to go or what he/she wants to eat, then decide where the two of you will go and what you will do.

B: On Wednesday you met A-san, who you are now having show you around Tokyo. Decide where to go together.

2.

A: You are back at work after a weeklong holiday. Talk to B-san about your time off (think about what you did on your own). B-san is also taking some time off next week, so ask about his/her upcoming plans.

B: Ask A-san questions like where he/she went for the holiday and what he/she did. Also talk with A-san about your plans for the time off you are taking next week (think about what you will do on your own).

113

Do you remember?

Use the phrases you have studied in this unit in situations ①–③ below.

①

What are you doing …?

I want to ….

②

ABC Company

Where …?

I'm going to ….

③

What did you do?

Yesterday, I ….

Phrases For This Unit

Unit Phrases

● 美術館に行きます。
びじゅつかん　い

Bijutsukan ni ikimasu.

I'm going to an art museum.

● 昨日はうちで日本語を
きのう　　　　　にほんご
勉強しました。
べんきょう

Kinō wa uchi de Nihon-go o benkyō shimashita.

I studied Japanese at home yesterday.

● すもうを見たいです。
み

Sumō o mitai desu.

I want to watch Sumo wresting.

Useful expressions

● おつかれさまです。

Otsukaresama desu.

Hello. / Goodbye. [a greeting used in the workplace instead of "Hello." or "Goodbye."]

● 一緒に行きましょう。
いっしょ　い

Issho ni ikimashō.

Let's go together.

● これから

korekara

from now

● [Place] で [verb]

[Place] de [verb]

[verb] at [place]

● [Person] と [verb]

[Person] to [verb]

[verb] with a [person]

Check!

Now I can...

☐ Talk about plans and what you are about to do

☐ Ask about things that have happened and places

people have been to

☐ Talk about interests and wants

Remember and Use!

● Verb Conjugations (masu-form) ●

	Non-past	Past
Affirmative	＿＿＿ます ＿＿＿masu	＿＿＿ました ＿＿＿mashita
Negative	＿＿＿ません ＿＿＿masen	＿＿＿ませんでした ＿＿＿masendeshita

→ See p.171, Grammar

● " ＿＿＿ni ＿＿＿masu" Verbs ●

[place / person]に＿＿＿ます　　[place / person] ni ＿＿＿masu

go 行きます／ikimasu 行く／iku	come 来ます／kimasu 来る／kuru
return / go home 帰ります／kaerimasu 帰る／kaeru	meet 会います／aimasu 会う／au

→ See Appendix, Verb Conjugation List

1. Make affirmative and negative sentences in different tenses using a noun with the particle "ni".

Ex.　来週、アメリカに帰ります。
らいしゅう　　　　　　　　　かえ
Raishū, Amerika **ni** kaerimasu.　　　　I'm going back to America next week.

2. Make and answer yes-or-no questions and then answer them.

Ex.　Q: 昨日、友だちに会いましたか。
きのう　　　　　　あ
Kinō, tomodachi **ni** aimashita ka.　　　Did you meet with a friend yesterday?

A: はい、会いました。／いいえ、会いませんでした。
あ　　　　　　　　　　あ
Hai, aimashita. / Iie, aimasendeshita.　Yes, I did. / No, I didn't.

3. Make questions using the word "itsu" (= when) and answer them.

Ex.　Q: いつ日本に来ましたか。
にほん　き
Itsu Nihon ni kimashita ka.　　　　　When did you come to Japan?

A: 去年の８月に*来ました。／先月に来ました。
きょねん　がつ　き　　　　　せんげつ　き
Kyonen no 8-gatsu **ni** kimashita. / Sengetsu ni kimashita.　　Last August. / Last month.

＊ When answering a "when" question, some time words require the particle **"ni"**, but not all do.

→ See p.104, Calendar

● "___o ___masu" Verbs ●

[object]を_____ます　　[object] o ____masu	
eat 食べます／tabemasu 食べる／taberu	drink 飲みます／nomimasu 飲む／nomu
look, see, watch 見ます／mimasu 見る／miru	read 読みます／yomimasu 読む／yomu
buy 買います／kaimasu 買う／kau	listen, hear 聞きます／kikimasu 聞く／kiku
take photos (写真を)撮ります／ (shashin o) torimasu 撮る／toru	study 勉強します／ benkyō shimasu 勉強する／benkyō suru

1. Make affirmative and negative sentences in different tenses using a noun with the particle "o".

Ex.　昨日、日本のテレビを見ました。
Kinō, Nihon no terebi **o** mimashita.　　I watched Japanese TV yesterday.

2. Make questions using verbs and answer them.

Ex.　Q: 昨日、ビールを飲みましたか。
Kinō, biru **o** nomimashita ka.　　Did you drink beer yesterday?

A: はい、飲みました。／いいえ、飲みませんでした。
Hai, nomimashita. / Iie, nomimasen deshita.　　Yes, I did. / No, I didn't.

3. Make questions using the phrase "doko de" (= where at) and answer them.

Ex.　Q: どこでそのカメラを買いましたか。
Doko de sono kamera **o** kaimashita ka.　　Where did you buy that camera?

A: 秋葉原で買いました。
Akihabara de kaimashita　　At Akihabara.

117

Good to Know

① Point card service

Japanese stores often have point cards, and cashiers will ask customers for their point card when they make a purchase. Some shops offer gifts or discounts if a certain amount of points are accrued. Here is a sample conversation.

Clerk:	Do you have point card?	Point kādo, omochi desu ka.
Customer:	No, I don't.	Arimasen.
Clerk:	Would you like to make one?	O-tsukuri shimasu ka.
Customer:	No thanks. / Yes, please.	Kekkō desu. / Onegai shimasu.

→ See p.90 for how to request gift wrapping or delivery.

· ·

② "Kekkō desu."

The phrase "kekkō desu." was introduced in Unit 4 as a way to "No, thank you," but originally means "It's fine the way it is" or "That way is fine." "Kekkō desu." can be used as a way to grant a person permission to do something (i.e. "The way you want to do it is fine."), but can also be used to make a refusal (= "No, thank you.").

Because this expression is used frequently and in a variety of situations, even native speakers of Japanese are sometimes unsure of its meaning.

A general rule of thumb is that the phrase "[**Noun**] de kekkō desu." is used to give permission, while "[**Noun**] wa kekkō desu." is used to refuse something unnecessary.

Ex.

Q: We only have tea, but would you like some?

A: Kekkō desu.

1. Ocha <u>de</u> kekkō desu. = Tea would be fine.
2. Ocha <u>wa</u> kekkō desu. = I'm fine without tea.

→ See p.58, Unit 4 and p.72, Unit 5.

How do you like living in Japan?

日本の生活はどうですか。
にほん　　せい　かつ
Nihon no seikatsu wa dō desu ka.

Talking about impressions

感想を言う

GOALS FOR UNIT 9

- Talk about your life in Japan

- Talk about your impression of things that happened in the past

Phrase 1 — Talk about your impression of something.

日本の生活はどうですか。
にほん　せいかつ

Track 65

Nihon no seikatsu wa dō desu ka. How do you like living in Japan?

NOTE " ____ wa dō desu ka." means "How is ____ ?" or "How do you like ____ ?" and can be used to ask someone what they think of something.

Ex.

田中　：日本の生活はどうですか。
たなか　にほん　せいかつ

ジョン：楽しいです。
たの

Tanaka ： <u>Nihon no seikatsu</u> **wa dō desu ka.**
Jon 　　： Tanoshii desu.

Tanaka ： How do you like living in Japan?
John 　　： It's fun.

Practice A-1

_____です。

Make sentences ending in " _____ **desu**" using the words below.

楽しい ☺ たの tanoshii fun /enjoyable	おもしろい ☺ omoshiroi fun/interesting	おいしい ☺ oishii dilicious/tasty
高い たか takai expensive/high	安い やす yasui cheap	むずかしい ☹ muzukashii difficult
いい ☺ ii good	便利 ☺ べんり benri convenient	きれい ☺ kirei clean/beautiful

120

_____ はどうですか。
Make questions using the following words with the phrase " _____ **wa dō desu ka.**"

日本の生活 に ほん　せい かつ Nihon no seikatsu life in Japan	日本料理 に ほんりょうり Nihon ryōri Japanese food	日本語 に ほん ご Nihon-go the Japanese language	今住んでいるところ いま す ima sundeiru tokoro the place where you/I live now

Put the words from Practice A-1 or A-2 in <　> and practice having a conversation.

田中
た なか ：ジョンさん、^A-2 〈日本の生活〉はどうですか。
にほん　せいかつ

ジョン ：(すごく) ^A-1 〈楽しい〉です。
た の

田中
た なか ：そうですか。^A-2 〈今住んでいるところ〉はどうですか。
いま す

ジョン ：(とても) ^A-1 〈便利〉ですよ。
べん り

Tanaka : Jon-san, ^A-2 < Nihon no seikatsu > wa
dō desu ka.

Jon : (Sugoku) ^A-1 < tanoshii > desu.

Tanaka : Sō desu ka. ^A-2 < Ima sundeiru tokoro >
wa dō desu ka.

Jon : (Totemo) ^A-1 < benri > desu yo.

> Tanaka : John-san, how do you like living in Japan?
> John : It's really fun.
> Tanaka : How's the place where you're living right
> now?
> John : It's very convenient.

MEMO

すごく ／ sugoku ／ very/extremely [casual]

とても ／ totemo ／ very [polite]

Phrase 2　Talk about your impression of something that happened in the past.

旅行はどうでしたか。
りょこう

Ryokō **wa dō deshita ka.**　　**How was** your trip?

Track
66

NOTE　"**Dō deshita ka**" is the past tense of "**dō desu ka**" and is used to ask a person for their impression of something that has already happened.
→ See the MEMO on p.123 for the past tense of different adjectives.

Ex.

田中　：旅行はどうでしたか。
たなか　りょこう

ジョン：よかったです。

Tanaka : <u>Ryokō</u> **wa dō deshita ka?**

Jon　　: Yokatta desu.

> Tanaka : How was your trip?
> John　　: It was good.

A-1　＿＿＿はどうでしたか。
Use the following words with the phrase "＿＿＿ **wa dō deshita ka.**"

旅行 りょこう ryokō trip	パーティー pāthī party	飲み会 の　かい nomikai drinking party at izakaya*	週末 しゅうまつ shūmatsu weekend

＊ izakaya = Japanese-style pub

A-2　＿＿＿です。
Answer the questions in Practice A-1 with a sentence ending in "＿＿＿ **desu.**"

よかった yokatta (it was) good	楽しかった たの tanoshikatta (it was) fun/enjoyable	おもしろかった omoshirokatta (it was) fun/interesting
すばらしかった subarashikatta (it was) wonderful	つまらなかった tsumaranakatta (it was) boring	いそがしかった isogashikatta (it was) busy

_____でした。

Answer the questions in Practice A-1 with sentences ending in "_____ **deshita.**"

まあまあ	ひま	大変
māmā	hima	たい へん
		taihen
(it was) so-so	(it was) free/not busy	(it was) terrible/hard/tough

Put words from Practice A-1, A-2, or A-3 in < > and practice having a conversation.
Use positive adjectives in ① and negative adjectives in ②.

①

田中：ジョンさん、^A-1〈旅行〉はどうでしたか。
たなか　　　　　　　りょこう

ジョン：^A-2〈楽しかった〉です。
　　　　　　たの

田中：それはよかったですね。
たなか

Tanaka : Jon-san, ^A-1< ryokō > wa dō deshita ka?
Jon　　: ^A-2< Tanoshikatta> desu.
Tanaka : Sore wa yokatta desu ne.

Tanaka : John-san, how was your trip?
Jon　　: It was fun.
Tanaka : I'm glad to hear that.

②

田中：ジョンさん、^A-1〈旅行〉はどうでしたか。
たなか　　　　　　　りょこう

ジョン：^A-2_A-3〈つまらなかった〉です／でした。

田中：そうですか。
たなか

Tanaka : Jon-san, ^A-1< ryoko > wa dō deshita ka?
Jon　　: ^A-2_A-3< Tsumaranakatta > desu/deshita.
Tanaka : Sō desu ka.

Tanaka : Jon-san, how was your trip?
John　 : It was boring.
Tanaka : Was it?

MEMO

それはよかったですね。／Sore wa yokatta desu ne.／That's good. / I'm glad to hear that.

*There are two types of adjectives in Japanese, i-adjectives and na-adjectives, both of which conjugate differently. Practice A-2 describes i-adjectives, while na-adjectives are taken up in Practice A-3.／→ See p.129

Practice having a conversation by replacing the words (1)–(5) with the words below. You can expand part of the conversation using the information on the right page.

佐藤 :(1)週末はどうでしたか。

カレン :すごく (2)楽しかったです。

はじめて(3)京都に行きました。

京都の町はとてもよかったです。

佐藤 :そうですか。

(4)日本のお寺はどうですか。

カレン :とても (5)きれいです。

Satō : (1)Shūmatsu wa dō deshita ka.

Karen : Sugoku (2)tanoshikatta desu.

Hajimete (3)Kyōto ni ikimashita.

Kyōto no machi wa totemo yokatta desu.

Satō : Sō desu ka.

(4)Nihon no otera wa dō desu ka.

Karen : Totemo (5)kirei desu.

---

①
(1) 昨日のパーティー   kinō no pāthī
(2) よかった   yokatta
(3) お好み焼きを食べました   okonomiyaki o tabemashita
(4) 日本料理   nihon-ryōri
(5) おいしい   oishii

②
(1) 休み   yasumi (=holiday/day off)
(2) おもしろかった   omoshirokatta
(3) カラオケに行きました   karaoke ni ikimashita
(4) 日本のカラオケ   nihon no karaoke
(5) すばらしい   subarashii (=wonderful)

③ Make your own conversation.

MEMO

はじめて／hajimete／for the first time

（お）寺／(o)tera／temple

Material

Look at the picture below and practice the conversation on the left page.

Ex.

カレン／Karen

京都に行きました。／Kyōto ni ikimashita.

- 町／machi (town)→よかった／yokatta
- 食べ物／tabemono (food)→おいしかった／oishikatta
- 京都の人／Kyōto no hito (People in Kyoto)→やさしかった
  ／yasashikatta (kind)

①

ジョン／Jon

お好み焼きを食べました。／okonomiyaki o tabemashita.

- お好み焼き／okonomiyaki→おいしかった／oishikatta
- お店／o-mise (shop)→小さかった／chiisakatta (small)
- 店の人／mise no hito (shop staff)→元気／genki (energetic)

②

クマール／Kumāru

カラオケに行きました。／karaoke ni ikimashita.

- 料金／ryōkin (fee, price)→高かった／takakatta
- 日本の歌／Nihon no uta (Japanese songs)→むずかしい／muzukashii
- カラオケ／karaoke→楽しい／tanoshii

③

You

＿＿＿＿＿＿ました。　mashita.

＿＿＿＿＿＿は wa ＿＿＿＿＿です／でした。desu/deshita.

→ See Appendix, Adjective Conjugation List

Listening

Listen to the conversation between the man and woman and choose the correct answer.

Q1 Two friends are talking after not seeing each other for a while
1. The woman enjoys her life in Japan.
2. The woman's apartment is very expensive.
3. Tokyo is very beautiful.

Q2 Two co-workers are talking at work
1. The food was neither good nor bad.
2. The party at the izakaya was neither good nor bad.
3. The party at the izakaya was fun.

Q3 Two friends are talking
1. The hotel was very crowded.
2. The man had a good trip.
3. The man was very busy on his trip.

Q4 Two friends are talking
1. Japanese temples are beautiful.
2. Japanese temples are expensive.
3. Japanese temples are old.

Role playing

Role play using the cards below.

1.

> **A:** You went on a trip last week. Tell B-san what you thought of your trip (think of the place you went on your own).

> **B:** Ask A-san questions about his/her trip, such as how was the weather, food, and hotel. Also, if possible, ask what A-san did on the trip.

2.

> **A:** You have recently moved to a town in Japan. Tell B-san what you think of it (talk about where you currently live).
> new=atarashii, town=machi,
> house/your place=uchi

> **B:** A-san has recently moved. Ask about A-san's new town (=atarashii machi), house (=uchi), and what life is like there.

Do you remember?

Use the phrases you have studied in this unit in situations ①–③ below.

①

Hawaii

How was …?

It was ….

②

How is …?

It's ….

③

Nomikai

How was …?

It was ….

Phrases for This Unit

Unit Phrases

- 日本の生活はどうですか。
  にほん　せいかつ

  Nihon no seikatsu wa dō desu ka.

  How do you like living in Japan?

- 旅行はどうでしたか。
  りょこう

  Ryokō wa dō deshita ka.

  How was your trip?

Useful expressions

- それはよかったですね。

  Sore wa yokatta desune.

  That's good. / I'm glad to hear that.

- すごく

  sugoku

  very [casual]

- とても

  totemo

  very [polite]

- はじめて

  hajimete

  for the first time

Check!

Now I can...

□ Talk about my life in Japan

□ Talk about my impression of things that

happen in the past

Remember and Use!

● I-adjective conjugations ●

	Non-past	Past
Affirmative	＿＿＿いです ＿＿＿i desu	＿＿＿かったです ＿＿＿katta desu
Negative	＿＿＿くないです ＿＿＿kunai desu	＿＿＿くなかったです ＿＿＿kunakatta desu

→ *See p.176, Grammar*

NOTE

The i-adjective "いい ii" conjugates irregularly.

	Non-past	Past
Affirmative	いいです ii desu	よかったです yokatta desu
Negative	よくないです yokunai desu	よくなかったです yokunakatta desu

● Basic i-adjectives 10 ●

hot あつい atsui		cold [weather] 寒い さむ samui	
big 大きい おお ōkii		small 小さい ちい chiisai	
expensive / high 高い たか takai		cheap 安い やす yasui	
difficult むずかしい muzukashii	easy / kind やさしい yasashii	fun / interesting おもしろい omoshiroi	delicious / tasty おいしい oishii

→ *See Appendix, Adjective Condugation List*

● Na-adjective conjugations ●

	Non-past	Past
Affirmative	_____です _____desu	_____でした _____deshita
Negative	_____じゃありません _____ja arimasen	_____じゃありませんでした _____ja arimasendeshita

● Basic na-adjectives 4 ●

convenient 便利 benri	clean / beautiful きれい kirei	quiet 静か shizuka	energetic / fine 元気 genki

1. Make affirmative and negative sentences in different tenses.

Ex. 日本語はむずかしくないです。 Nihon-go wa muzukashikunai desu.

京都は静かでした。 Kyōto wa shizuka deshita.

2. Make questions using adjectives and answer them.

Ex. Q: 東京はあついですか。 Tōkyō wa atsui desu ka.

A: はい、あついです。 Hai, atsui desu.

いいえ、あつくないです。 Iie, atsukunai desu.

Q: ホテルはきれいでしたか。 Hoteru wa kirei deshita ka.

A: はい、きれいでした。 Hai, kirei deshita.

いいえ、きれいじゃありませんでした。 Iie, kirei ja arimasendeshita.

3. Have a free conversation about the topics below. → *See pp.120-123 and Appendix*

東京 Tōkyō Tokyo	会社 kaisha Your company	うち uchi Your house	日本語の先生 Nihon-go no sensei Japanese teachers
昨日の晩ごはん kinō no bangohan What you had for dinner last night	Languages you have studied	Places you have been on	Places you have lived

What does that taste like?

それ、どんな味ですか。

Sore, donna aji desu ka.

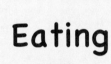

Eating

食事

GOALS FOR UNIT 10

- Understand and use taste words

- Say what a food probably tastes like based on its appearance

- Politely refuse foods you do not like/do not eat

Phrase 1　Ask what something tastes like.

それ、**どんな味ですか**。

Sore, donna aji desu ka.

Track 72

What does that **taste like?**

NOTE　**"Donna"** and **"aji"** mean **"what kind of"** and **"taste"**, and are used to ask what something tastes like.

Ex.

ジョン ：それ、**どんな味ですか**。

田中 ：<u>あまい</u>**です**。おいしいですよ。
たなか

Jon ： Sore, **donna aji desu ka.**

Tanaka ： <u>Amai</u> **desu**. Oishii desu yo.

John ： What does that taste like?

Tanaka ： It's sweet. It tastes good.

Practice A

_____ です。
Answer the question **"Donna aji desu ka."** using a phrase that ends in **"_____ desu."**

あまい amai sweet	からい karai spicy / hot	すっぱい suppai sour
しょっぱい shoppai salty	にがい nigai bitter	油っこい あぶら aburakkoi oily
あまからい amakarai sweet and salty	さっぱりした味 あじ sapparishita aji refreshing taste	おもしろい味 あじ omoshiroi aji interesting taste

おいしい	おいしくない	味があまりない
oishii	oishikunai	aji ga amarinai
delicious/good	not delicious/not good	doesn't taste like much

Practice B
Put the words from Practice A in < > and practice having a conversation.
→ See Pre-text p. i - iv for additional food words.

– At a restaurant –

クマール : それ、どんな味ですか。

田中 : 〈あまい〉ですよ。食べてみますか。

クマール : じゃ、食べてみます。／いいえ、いいです。

Kumāru : Sore, donna aji desu ka

Tanaka : < Amai > desu yo. Tabete mimasu ka.

Kumāru : Ja, tabete mimasu. / Iie, ii desu.

Kumar: What does that taste like?

Tanaka: It's sweet. Would you like to try it?

Kumar: I think I will. / No, that's okay.

MEMO

食べてみますか。／Tabete mimasu ka. ／Would you like to try it? [used for food]

食べてみます。／Tabete mimasu. ／I'll have a taste. / I'll try it. [used for food]

いいえ、いいです。／Iie, ii desu. ／No, that's okay.

Say what a food probably tastes like based on its appearance.

おいし**そうですね**。

Oishisō desu ne.

That looks delicious.

Track
73

NOTE "_____ **sō desu.**" means "(That) **looks** _____." and can be used to describe something based on its physical appearance. The final "**i**" or "**na**" of an adjective is removed before being attached to "**sō desu**".

Ex.

ジョン ：おいし**そう**ですね。

田中 ：そうですね。
たなか

Jon ： Oishi**sō desu ne.**
Tanaka ： Sō desu ne.

John ： That looks delicious.
Tanaka ： It really does.

_____そうです。
Change the "**i**" portion of the follwing words to "____ **sō desu.**"

おいし（い）	あつ（い）	から（い）
oishi(i)	atsu(i)	kara(i)
delicious	hot	spicy/hot
あま（い）	まず（い）	すっぱ（い）
ama(i)	mazu(i)	suppa(i)
sweet	gross/bad	sour
やわらか（い）	油っこ（い） あぶら	体によさ* からだ
yawaraka(i)	aburakko(i)	karada ni yosa*
soft	oily	healthy/good for you

* The adjective "**ii**" (good) conjugates exceptionally to "**yosasō desu**".

Practice B Put the words from Practice A in < > and practice having a conversation.

- Looking at a menu at a restaurant -

佐藤(さとう) ：何(なん)にしますか。これはどうですか。

ジョン ：うーん、ちょっと〈油(あぶら)っこ〉そうですね。

佐藤(さとう) ：じゃ、これはどうですか。

ジョン ：うん、〈おいし〉そうですね。

佐藤(さとう) ：じゃ、これにしましょう。

Satō ： Nan ni shimasu ka. Kore wa dō desu ka.

Jon ： Ūn, chotto < aburakko > sō desu ne.

Satō ： Ja, kore wa dō desu ka.

Jon ： Un, < oishi >sō desu ne.

Satō ： Ja, kore ni shimashō.

Sato ： What should we get? How about this?

John ： Hm, that looks a little oily.

Sato ： Then how about this?

John ： Yeah, that looks good.

Sato ： Okay, let's get this, then.

MEMO

何(なん)にしますか。／Nan ni shimasu ka.／What are we/you going to have?

これはどうですか。／Kore wa dō desu ka.／How about this?

ちょっと～そうですね。／Chotto …sō desu ne.／It looks a little ….

これにしましょう。／Kore ni shimashō.／Let's have this.

Phrase 3 — Politely refuse foods you do not like.

豚肉はちょっと……。
ぶたにく

Butaniku **wa chotto**…….   **I can't really eat** pork.

> NOTE   "____**wa chotto**……" can be used to convey negative feelings, with an implication that you don't like or don't want to do something. Follow a **"wa chotto**……" statement with a reason followed by "____**nan desu**" to provide a polite explanation.

Ex.

田中 ：これ、おいしいですよ。
たなか

クマール：すみません。豚肉はちょっと……。
ぶたにく
ベジタリアンなんです。

Tanaka ： Kore, oishii desu yo.
Kumāru ： Sumimasen. Butaniku **wa chotto**…….
Bejitarian nan desu.

> Tanaka : This is really good.
> Kumar : I'm sorry, but I can't eat pork.
> (The thing is) I'm a vegetarian.

Practice A-1

____はちょっと……。
Use the following words with the phrase " ____**wa chotto**……."

豚肉	牛肉	卵	生もの
ぶた にく	ぎゅうにく	たまご	なま
butaniku	gyūniku	tamago	namamono
pork	beef	egg	raw food
わさび	シーフード	からいもの	あまいもの
wasabi	shīfūdo	karai mono	amai mono
wasabi → *See Pre-text p.iv*	seafood	spicy things	sweet things

Practice A-2

Explain why you can't eat the foods in Practice A-1 using the following words with the phrase
_____**nandesu.**

ベジタリアン	アレルギー	苦手 にが て	宗教でだめ しゅうきょう
bejitarian	arerugī	nigate	shūkyō de dame
vegitarian	allergy	not good at	for religious reasons

Practice B

Put the words from Practice A-1 or A-2 in < > and practice having a conversation.

田中 ：これ、どうですか。
たなか

クマール：^{A-1}〈豚肉〉ですか。^{A-1}〈豚肉〉はちょっと……。
　　　　　　ぶたにく　　　　　　　　ぶたにく

田中 ：そうなんですか。
たなか

クマール：はい、^{A-2}〈苦手〉なんです。
　　　　　　　　　　にが て

Tanaka　 : Kore, dō desu ka.
Kumāru　: ^{A-1}< Butaniku > desu ka.
　　　　　　^{A-1}< Butaniku > wa chotto…….
Tanaka　 : Sō nan desu ka.
Kumāru　: Hai, ^{A-2}< nigate > nan desu.

Tanaka : How about this?
Kumar　: Is it pork? I can't eat pork.
Tanaka : Oh really?
Kumar　: Yes, I don't care for the taste.

MEMO

そうなんですか。／Sō nan desu ka.／Oh really? / Is that so? [indicates a feeling of surprise]

Dialogue

Replace the words in (1) – (4) below and practice having a conversation.

ジョン ：(1)<u>肉じゃが</u>って、どんな味ですか。

鈴木 ：(2)<u>あまい</u>ですよ。おいしいです。

ジョン ：そうですか。　Pointing at another food

これは(3)<u>からそう</u>ですね。

鈴木 ：ええ、(4)<u>からい</u>ですよ。

ジョン ：そうですか。(4)<u>からい</u>ものは

ちょっと……。

苦手なんです。

鈴木 ：じゃ、他のにしましょう。これは？

ジョン ：おいしそうですね。

鈴木 ：じゃ、これにしましょう。

Jon 　：(1) <u>Nikujaga</u> tte donna aji desu ka.

Suzuki ：(2) <u>Amai</u> desu yo. Oishii desu.

Jon 　：Sō desu ka.　Pointing at another food

Kore wa (3) <u>karasō</u> desu ne.

Suzuki ：Ee, (4) <u>karai</u> desu yo.

Jon 　：Sō desu ka. (4) <u>Karai</u> mono wa

chotto... .

Nigate nan desu.

Suzuki ：Ja, hoka no ni shimashō. Kore wa?

Jon 　：Oishisō desu ne.

Suzuki ：Ja, kore ni shimashō.

---

① (1) こんにゃく　　　　　　　　　konnyaku (→ See Pre-text p.iv)
　　(2) 味があまりない　　　　　　aji ga amari nai
　　(3) 油っこそう　　　　　　　　aburakkosō
　　(4) 油っこい　　　　　　　　　aburakkoi

---

② (1) うめぼし　　　　　　　　　umeboshi (→ See Pre-text p.iii)
　　(2) すっぱい　　　　　　　　　suppai
　　(3) あまそう　　　　　　　　　amasō
　　(4) あまい　　　　　　　　　　amai

MEMO

〜って／...tte → See p.55 MEMO

もの／mono／thing(s)

他のにしましょう。／Hoka no ni shimashō.／Let's have something else/another one.

これにしましょう。／Kore ni shimashō.／Let's have this.

Listening

Listen to the conversation between the man and woman and choose the correct answer.

Q1   Pointing at the food on the table

1. The food is spicy.
2. The food is refreshing.
3. The food is sour.

Q2   Looking at the food on the next table

1. The man wants to order beef.
2. The man doesn't like beef.
3. The man is going to try the beef.

Q3   Looking at a menu

1. The salad looks oily.
2. The salad looks light.
3. The salad looks healthy.

Q4   Looking at a menu

1. They will order spicy food.
2. They will not order spicy food.
3. They will not order anything.

Role playing

Role play using the cards below

A: You are at an izakaya with B-san. Ask what dish B-san recommends, then ask what it tastes like, give a reason why you cannot eat it, and refuse the food.

B: You are at an izakaya with A-san. Look at the menu in the pre-text and recommend your favorite food.

Do you remember?

Use the phrases you have studied in this unit in situations ①–③ below.

①

What ⋯ taste like?

↑
umeboshi

②

That looks ⋯.

③

How about ⋯?   I can't ⋯.

Phrases for This Unit

Unit Phrases

● それ、どんな味ですか。　　Sore, donna aji desu ka.　　What does it taste like?

● おいしそうですね。　　Oishisō desu ne.　　It looks delicious.

● 豚肉はちょっと……。　　Butaniku wa chotto…….　　I can't really eat pork.

Useful expressions

● 食べてみますか。　　Tabete mimasu ka.　　Would you like to try it? [used with food]

● 食べてみます。　　Tabete mimasu.　　I'll have a taste. [used with food]

● いいえ、いいです。　　Iie, ii desu.　　No, that's okay.

● これにしましょう。　　Kore ni shimashō.　　Let's have this.

● 苦手なんです。　　Nigate nan desu.　　I'm not good at it. [a common refusal]

● そうなんですか。　　Sō nan desu ka.　　Oh, really? / Is that so? [indicates surprise]

Check!

Now I can...

☐ Understand and use taste words

☐ Say what a food probably tastes like based on its appearance

☐ Politely refuse foods I do not like/do not eat

Good to Know

Common menu "kanji"

Ingredients ··································

1. 豚肉
butaniku／pork

2. 牛肉
gyūniku／beef

3. 鶏肉（鳥肉）
toriniku／chicken

4. 卵（玉子）
tamago／egg

5. 魚
sakana／fish

6. 貝
kai／shellfish

7. 野菜
yasai／vegetables

8. 豆腐
tōfu／tofu

Cooking Method ··································

1. 焼く
ya-ku／grill

2. 炒める
ita-meru／stir-fry

3. 揚げる
a-geru／deep fry

4. 蒸す
mu-su／steam

5. 煮る
ni-ru／boil, simmer

6. 温かい
atata-kai
／warm

7. 冷たい
tsume-tai
／cold

It's nice weather today, isn't it?

今日はいい天気ですね。
きょう　　　てん　き
Kyō wa ii tenki desu ne.

Socializing I - Making Small Talk
世間話をする

GOALS FOR UNIT 11

- Start a conversation after saying hello

- Make simple small talk by asking about a person's family and job

- Learn other ways to say goodbye than *sayonara*

今日はいい天気ですね。
きょう　　　　　てんき

Kyō wa ii tenki **desu ne.**

It's nice weather **today, isn't it?**

<u>NOTE</u> "____desu ne." is frequently used when the speaker feels like the listener will agree with what he or she is saying.

Ex.

ジョン ：今日は<u>いい天気</u>ですね。
　　　　きょう　　てんき

田中　 ：そうですね。
たなか

Jon　　 : **Kyō wa** <u>ii tenki</u> **desu ne.**

Tanaka : Sō desu ne.

John　　 : It's nice weather today, isn't it?

Tanaka : It sure is.

今日は_____ですね。
きょう

Use the following words with the phrase " **Kyō wa _____ desu ne.**"

いい天気 てんき ii tenki good weather	嫌な天気 いや　てんき iyana tenki bad weather	雨 あめ ame rain
蒸し暑い む　　あつ mushi atsui humid	風が強い かぜ　つよ kaze ga tsuyoi windy	暑い あつ atsui hot
寒い さむ samui cold	暖かい* あたた atatakai* warm	涼しい すず suzushii cool

* "**Atatakai**" is frequently abbreviated to "**attakai**" in casual conversation.

Practice B Put the words from Practice A in < > and practice having a conversation.

-John-san runs into the janitor of his apartment building on his way out-

ジョン　：おはようございます。

管理人　：おはようございます。
かんりにん

ジョン　：今日は〈いい天気〉ですね。／今日も〈いい天気〉ですね。
　　　　　きょう　　　　てんき　　　　　　きょう　　　　　てんき

管理人　：そうですね。最近／毎日、〈暑い〉ですね。
かんりにん　　　　　　　さいきん　まいにち　あつ

ジョン　：本当ですね。じゃ、いってきます。
　　　　　ほんとう

管理人　：いってらっしゃい。
かんりにん

Jon	: Ohayō gozaimasu.
Kanri-nin	: Ohayō gozaimasu.
Jon	: Kyō wa < ii tenki > desu ne.
	/ Kyō mo <ii tenki> desu ne.
Kanri-nin	: Sō desu ne.
	Saikin / Mainichi < atsui > desu ne.
Jon	: Hontō desu ne. Ja, ittekimasu.
Kanri-nin	: Itterasshai.

John	: Good morning.
Janitor	: Good morning.
John	: It's nice weather today, isn't it?
	/ The weather is nice again today, isn't it?
Janitor	: It sure is.
	It's been hot lately/everyday.
John	: It sure has. See you later.
Janitor	: Have a nice day.

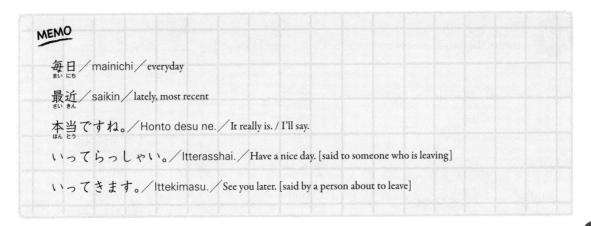

MEMO

毎日／mainichi／everyday
まいにち

最近／saikin／lately, most recent
さいきん

本当ですね。／Honto desu ne.／It really is. / I'll say.
ほんとう

いってらっしゃい。／Itterasshai.／Have a nice day. [said to someone who is leaving]

いってきます。／Ittekimasu.／See you later. [said by a person about to leave]

最近、仕事はどうですか。
さいきん　し ごと

Saikin, shigoto **wa dō desu ka.**   How has your job **been lately?**

NOTE "Saikin _____ wa dō desu ka" means "How has [topic] been lately?" The phrase "Saikin dō desu ka." is also often used to ask a person how they have been.

Ex.

佐藤 ：最近、仕事はどうですか。
さとう 　さいきん　し ごと

ジョン ：順調です。
　　　　じゅんちょう

Satō : **Saikin** shigoto **wa dō desu ka.**

Jon : Junchō desu.

> Sato : How has your work been lately?
> John : It's been going well.

A-1

最近_____はどうですか。
さいきん

Use the following words with the phrase " **Saikin _____ wa dō desu ka.**"

仕事 し ごと shigoto job / work	調子 ちょう し chōshi condition	ご家族 か ぞく go-kazoku (your) family	学校／勉強 がっ こう　べん きょう gakkō / benkyō school / study

A-2

_____です。

Answer the questions above with the following words followed by "_____ **desu.**"

順調 じゅんちょう junchō going well	元気 げん き genki fine	楽しい たの tanoshii fun / enjoyable
忙しい いそが isogashii busy	まあまあ māmā so-so	大変 たい へん taihen hard / tough

Practice B

Put the words from Practice A-1 and A-2 in < > and practice having a conversation.

-John-san runs into his former teacher-

ジョン :先生、お久しぶりです。

前の先生 :あ、ジョンさん。お久しぶりです。お元気ですか。

ジョン :はい、おかげさまで。

前の先生 :最近 ^{A-1}〈仕事〉はどうですか。

ジョン :おかげさまで ^{A-2}〈順調〉です。

先生はいかがですか。

前の先生 :私も ^{A-2}〈順調〉ですよ。／^{A-2}〈忙しい〉ですよ。

Jon	: Sensei, ohisashiburi desu.
Mae no sensei	: A, Jon-san, ohisashiburi desu. O-genki desu ka.
Jon	: Hai, okagesama de.
Mae no sensei	: Saikin, ^{A-1}< shigoto > wa dō desuka.
Jon	: Okagasama de ^{A-2}< junchō > desu. Sensei wa ikaga desu ka.
Mae no sensei	: Watashi mo ^{A-2}< junchō > desu yo. / ^{A-2}< Isogashii > desu yo.

John	: Sensei, I haven't seen you for quite a while.
Former teacher	: Oh, John-san, it has been a long time. How are you doing?
John	: I'm doing well, knock on wood.
Former teacher	: How has your work been?
John	: It's been going well, fortunately. How about you?
Former teacher	: I've been well. / I've been busy.

MEMO

お久しぶりです。／Ohisashiburi desu.／Long time no see. / It's been a while.

おかげさまで。／Okagesama de.／Thanks to you. [an expression of gratitude indebting a person for your success, health, and wellbeing; often used as a term of greeting to strengthen human relations even when no favors have been exchanged]

いかがですか。／Ikaga desu ka.／How about you? [a polite way of saying "dō desu ka."]

Phrase 3   Use natural-sounding Japanese when saying goodbye.

じゃ、また。

Ja, mata.   **See you** later.

> NOTE   **"Ja"**, a contraction of **"dewa"**, is used to mean **"well"** or **"then"** to end a topic of conversation. **"Ja"** is also used in modern Japanese as a way to say goodbye, akin to **"see you"** in English.

Ex.

ジョン ：**じゃ、**<u>また</u>。

佐藤 ：じゃ、また来週。
さとう　　　　　　らいしゅう

Jon   : **Ja,** <u>mata</u>.
Satō   : Ja, mata raishū.

> John : See you later.
> Sato : See you next week.

Practice A

じゃ、_____ 。
Use the following words with the phrase **"Ja, _____ ."**

また	また来週	また今度
mata	mata raishū	mata kondo
See you (later).	See you next week.	See you next time.
また後で*1	お大事に	気をつけて
mata atode*1	o-daiji ni	ki o tsukete
See you later.	Get well soon.	Take care.
（お先に*2）失礼します	また連絡します	お元気で
(o-saki ni*2) shitsurei shimasu	mata renraku shimasu	o-genki de
Goodbye.	I'll be in touch (soon).	Be well. / Take care of yourself.

＊1 The phrase **"mata ato de"** is used when you expect to see a person later that day or within a similar time interval.

＊2 The phrase **"o-saki ni"** means **"before you."** **"Shitsurei shimasu"** is often used as a way to say goodbye when leaving work before other people or when exiting a meeting, and is frequently shortened to **"o-saki ni"** in casual conversation.

 Practice B Use words from practice A in <   > to practice having a conversation.
＊ Choose words suitable for the situation.

① Leaving work before co-worker Tanaka-san

ジョン ：じゃ、〈   　〉。

田中　：おつかれさまでした。
た なか

Jon　　 : Ja, <　　　>.
Tanaka : Otsukaresama deshita.

> John　　: See you <　>.
> Tanaka : Goodbye.

② To a friend who is ill

ジョン ：じゃ、〈   　〉。

佐藤　：ありがとう。
さ とう

Jon　 : Ja, <　　　>.
Satō　: Arigatō.

> John　 : <　>.
> Sato　: Thank you.

③ To a friend you will not see for a long time

ジョン ：じゃ、〈   　〉。

友達　：〈   　〉。
ともだち

Jon　　　　 : Ja, <　　　>.
Tomodachi : <　　　>.

> John　 : <　>.
> Friend : <　>.

 MEMO
おつかれさまでした。／Otsukaresama deshita. ／Good work today. / Goodbye.
["Otsukaresama deshita" is a greeting used in the workplace instead of "Goodbye."]

Dialogue

Have a practice conversation replacing the words in (1) - (5).

- At a party -

田中
（たなか） ：こんにちは。今日は(1)寒いですね。
　　　　　　　　（きょう）　　（さむ）

クマール ：本当ですね。
　　　　　　（ほんとう）

　　　　　　最近、(2)お仕事はどうですか。
　　　　　　（さいきん）　（しごと）

田中
（たなか） ：(3)順調です。 クマールさんは？
　　　　　　（じゅんちょう）

クマール ：(4)忙しいです。
　　　　　　　　（いそが）

- Later -

クマール ：すみません、

　　　　　　今日はそろそろ帰ります。
　　　　　　（きょう）　　　　　　（かえ）

田中
（たなか） ：そうですか。じゃ、気をつけて。
　　　　　　　　　　　　　　　（き）

クマール ：じゃ、(5)また。

- At a party -

Tanaka　： Konnichiwa. Kyō wa (1)samui desu ne.

Kumāru　： Hontō desu ne.

　　　　　　Saikin, (2)o-shigoto wa dō desu ka.

Tanaka　： (3)Junchō desu. Kumāru-san wa?

Kumāru　： (4)Isogashii desu.

- Later -

Kumāru　： Sumimasen,

　　　　　　kyō wa sorosoro kaerimasu.

Tanaka　： Sō desu ka. Ja, ki o tsukete.

Kumāru　： Ja, (5)mata.

---

①
(1) 暑い （あつ）　　　　　　atsui
(2) 調子 （ちょうし）　　　　chōshi
(3) まあまあ　　　　　　　　māmā
(4) 私もまあまあ （わたし）　watashi mo māmā
(5) また来週 （らいしゅう）　mata raishū

②
(1) いやな天気 （てんき）　　iyana tenki
(2) ご家族 （かぞく）　　　　go-kazoku
(3) 元気 （げんき）　　　　　genki
(4) うちもみんな元気 （げんき）　uchi mo minna genki
(5) お先に失礼します （さき）（しつれい）　o-saki ni shitsurei shimasu

MEMO

そろそろ帰ります。／Sorosoro kaerimasu.／I have to leave now.
　　（かえ）

うちもみんな元気です。／Uchi mo minna genki desu.／Everyone at home is doing well.
　　　　　　　（げんき）

150

Listening

Listen to the conversation between the man and woman and choose the correct answer.

Q1 Two neighbors are talking in the morning
1. It's hot everyday.
2. It's cool everyday.
3. It's warm everyday.

Q3 At work
1. The woman is leaving now.
2. The man is leaving now.
3. The man and woman are meeting tomorrow.

Q2 Two colleagues from different departments are talking
1. The woman is busy.
2. The woman is not doing well.
3. The man is busy.

Q4 Two friends are talking after not seeing each other for a while
1. The man isn't doing too well.
2. The man is doing well.
3. The man is coming down with a cold.

Role playing

Role play using the cards below.

1.

A: You run into B-san, your former co-worker, whom you haven't seen for a long time. Ask B-san how his/her job and family have been.

B: You run into A-san, former co-worker, whom you haven't seen for a long time. Ask how A-san is doing.

2.

A: You run into your neighbor B-san on the street. Talk about how the weather has been recently and say goodbye.

B: You run into your neighbor A-san on the street. Say hello.

Do you remember?

Use the phrases you have studied in this unit in situations ①–③ below.

①

It's ….

②

How is …?

③

I hope ….

Phrases for This Unit

Unit Phrases

● 今日はいい天気ですね。
きょう　　　　　てんき

Kyō wa ii tenki desu ne.

It's nice weather today, isn't it?

● 最近、仕事はどうですか。
さいきん　しごと

Saikin shigoto wa dō desu ka.

How has your job been lately?

● じゃ、また。

Ja, mata.

See you later.

Useful expressions

● 本当ですね。
ほんとう

Hontō desu ne.

It really is. / I'll say.

● おつかれさまでした。

Otsukaresama deshita.

Good work today. / Goodbye.

● お久しぶりです。
ひさ

Ohisashiburi desu.

Long time no see. / It's been a while.

● そろそろ帰ります。
かえ

Sorosoro kaerimasu.

I have to leave now.

Check!

Now I can...

☐ Start a conversation after saying hello

☐ Make simple small talk by asking about a person's family and job

☐ Learn other ways to say goodbye than *sayonara*

One More Step

● Talking about the weather

3-gatsu Mar.	春 はる haru spring	
4-gatsu Apr.		
5-gatsu May		
6-gatsu Jun.	（梅雨） つゆ tsuyu rainy season	
7-gatsu Jul.	夏 なつ natsu summer	
8-gatsu Aug.		
9-gatsu Sep.	秋 あき aki autumn	
10-gatsu Oct.		
11-gatsu Nov.		
12-gatsu Dec.	冬 ふゆ fuyu winter	
1-gatsu Jan.		
2-gatsu Feb.		

あたたかい
atatakai
warm

さわやかですね。
Sawayaka desu ne.
It's nice(balmy) outside today.

蒸し暑い
む あつ
mushi atsui
humid

暑い
あつ
atsui
hot

涼しい
すず
suzushii
cool

気持ちいいですね。
き も
Kimochi ii desu ne.
It feels so nice.

寒い
さむ
samui
cold

晴れ
は
hare
sunny

くもり
kumori
cloudy

雨
あめ
ame
rain

雷
かみなり
kaminari
thunder

台風
たい ふう
taifū
typhoon

風
かぜ
kaze
wind

雪
ゆき
yuki
snow

→ See p.104, Calendar

Would you like to have a cup of tea?

お茶を飲みませんか。
Ocha o nomimasen ka.

Socializing II - Invitations -

誘う

GOALS FOR UNIT 12

- Talk about your own experiences and ask about those of others

- Invite a person to do or have something

- Accept and refuse invitations

Phrase 1 — Invite a friend or co-worker to do something.

お茶を飲み**ませんか**。
ちゃ　の

Ocha o nomimasen ka.　　　**Would you like to** have a cup of tea?

Track 88

NOTE The negative question form of a masu verb, **"[verb-stem]masen ka"**, means **"Would you like to [verb]?"** or **"Why don't you [verb]?"** and is used when inviting someone to do something with you.

Ex.

カレン ：鈴木さん、これから<u>お茶を飲み</u>**ませんか**。
　　　　すずき　　　　　　　ちゃ　の

鈴木 　：いいですね。そうしましょう。
すずき

Karen 　 : Suzuki-san, korekara <u>ocha o nomi</u>**masen ka**.
Suzuki : Ii desu ne. Sō shimashō.

> Karen 　 : Suzuki-san, would you like to have a cup of tea right now?
> Suzuki : Sounds good. Let's do it.

Practice A-1

_____ ませんか。

Change the **"masu"** portion of the follwing words to " _____ **masen ka**."

お茶を飲み（ます） ちゃ　の ocha o nomi(masu) have a cup of tea [lit. drink tea]	ボウリングをし（ます） bōringu o shi(masu) go bowling	ごはんを食べに行き（ます） た gohan o tabe ni iki(masu) go out to eat
映画を見（ます） えい が　み eiga o mi(masu) see a movie	飲みに行き（ます） の　い nomi ni iki(masu) go out for a drink	遊びに行き（ます） あそ　い asobi ni iki(masu) go out to have fun

Practice A-2

Add the following words to the phrases above to make invitations using **"___masen ka."**

これから korekara right now	今晩 こん ばん komban tonight	週末 しゅう まつ shūmatsu weekend	明日 あした ashita tomorrow → *See p.104, Calendar*

Put the words from Practice A-1 or A-2 in < > and practice having a conversation. Fill in [   ] with the name of a place.

① •••••••••••••••••••••••••••••••••••••

鈴木(すずき) ：ジョンさん、^{A-2}〈これから〉一緒(いっしょ)に^{A-1}〈お茶(ちゃ)を飲(の)み〉ませんか。

ジョン ：いいですね。どこに行(い)きましょうか。

鈴木(すずき) ：[   ]はどうですか。

ジョン ：いいですね。そうしましょう。

Suzuki : Jon-san, ^{A-2}< korekara > issho ni
^{A-1}< ocha o nomi > masen ka.

Jon : Ii desu ne. Doko ni ikimashō ka.

Suzuki : [   ] wa dō desu ka.

Jon : Ii desu ne. Sō shimashō.

Suzuki : Jon-san, would you like to get tea with me
right now?

John : That sounds nice. Where should we go?

Suzuki : How does [   ] sound?

John : That sounds great. Let's go there.

② •••••••••••••••••••••••••••••••••••••

鈴木(すずき) ：ジョンさん、^{A-2}〈明日(あした)〉一緒(いっしょ)に^{A-1}〈映画(えいが)を見(み)〉ませんか。

ジョン ：すみません、^{A-2}〈明日(あした)〉はちょっと……。

鈴木(すずき) ：そうですか。じゃ、また今度(こんど)。

ジョン ：すみません。また誘(さそ)ってください。

Suzuki : Jon-san, ^{A-2}< ashita > issho ni
^{A-1}< eiga o mi >masen ka.

Jon : Sumimasen, ^{A-2}< ashita > wa chotto......

Suzuki : Sō desu ka. Ja, mata kondo.

Jon : Sumimasen. Mata sasotte kudasai.

Suzuki : Jon-san, would you like to go see a movie
tomorrow?

John : I'm sorry, tomorrow's not good for me.

Suzuki : Okay. Well, next time, then.

John : Thanks. Please invite me again.

MEMO

どこに行(い)きましょうか。／Doko ni ikimashō ka.／Where should we go?

〜はどうですか。／... wa dō desu ka.／How about ...? / How does ... sound?

じゃ、また今度(こんど)。／Ja, mata kondo.／Well, next time, then.

〜はちょっと……。／... wa chotto....／... is no good for me.

また誘(さそ)ってください。／Mata sasotte kudasai.／Please invite/ ask me again. [Often said after
refusing an invitation]

温泉に行った**ことがありますか**。
おんせん　い

Onsen ni itta **koto ga arimasu ka.**

Have you ever been to an *onsen* (hot spring)?

Track 89

NOTE "**[Verb-ta] + koto ga arimasu**" means "(I) have [done...]" and is used to talk about one's experience. →*See p.173, Grammar: Ta-form*

Ex.

田中　：温泉に行った**ことがありますか**。
たなか　　おんせん　い

ジョン：はい、あります。よかったですよ。

Tanaka : Onsen ni itta **koto ga arimasu ka.**
Jon　　 : Hai, arimasu. Yokatta desu yo.

Tanaka : Have you ever been to an *onsen*?
John　　: Yes, I have. It was nice.

Practice A

[verb-ta]**ことがありますか**。
Use the following words with the phrase "**[verb-ta] koto ga arimasu ka.**"

温泉に行った おんせん　い onsen ni itta went to an *onsen* (hot spring)	カラオケに行った い karaoke ni itta went to karaoke	スノーボードをした sunō-bōdo o shita went snowboarding
花見をした はなみ hanami o shita went flower-viewing	日本の花火を見た にほん　はなび　み Nihon no hanabi o mita saw Japanese fireworks	歌舞伎を見た かぶき　み kabuki o mita saw kabuki → **See Appendix**
お好み焼きを食べた この　や　た okonomiyaki o tabeta ate okonomiyaki	焼酎を飲んだ しょうちゅう　の shōchū o nonda drank shochu	着物を着た きもの　き kimono o kita wore a kimono

Put the words from Practice A in < > and practice having a conversation. Fill in [ ] with an adjective. → See Unit 9.

① ●

佐藤 ：ジョンさん、〈温泉に行った〉ことがありますか。
<small>さとう</small>　　　　　　<small>おんせん</small>　<small>い</small>

ジョン：はい、あります。

佐藤 ：そうですか。どうでしたか。
<small>さとう</small>

ジョン：とても［よかったです］。

→ *See Appendix, Adjective Conjugation List*

Satō	: Jon-san, onsen ni itta koto ga ariamasu ka.
Jon	: Hai, arimasu.
Satō	: Sō desuka. Dō deshita ka.
Jon	: Totemo [yokatta desu].

Sato	: John-san, have you ever been to an onsen hot spring?
John	: Yes, I have.
Sato	: I see. How did you like it?
John	: It was really nice.

② ●

佐藤 ：ジョンさん、〈カラオケに行った〉ことがありますか。
<small>さとう</small>　　　　　　　　　　　<small>い</small>

ジョン：いいえ、ありません。

佐藤 ：じゃ、今度、一緒に行きませんか。
<small>さとう</small>　　<small>こんど</small>　<small>いっしょ</small>　<small>い</small>

ジョン：いいですね。そうしましょう。

Satō	: Jon-san, < karaoke ni itta >koto ga arimasu ka.
Jon	: Iie, arimasen.
Satō	: Ja, kondo, issho ni ikimasen ka.
Jon	: Ii desu ne. Sō shimashō.

Sato	: John-san, have you ever been to karaoke?
John	: No, I haven't.
Sato	: Oh, then would you like to go with me sometime?
John	: That sounds great. Let's do it.

MEMO

そうしましょう。／Sō shimashō.／Let's do that/it.

Dialogue

Replace the words (1) - (3) and put your own answers in < > to practice having a conversation. You can also use words and grammatical devices from Unit 8 to expand ▨▨▨ part of the conversation.

→ *See p.104, Calendar*

Expand your conversation

田中 ：クマールさん、いつ日本に来ましたか。

クマール：〈去年の9月〉に来ました。

....

田中 ：(1)花見をしたことがありますか。

クマール：いいえ、ありません。

田中 ：よかったら、日曜日に(2)一緒に(3)行きませんか。

クマール：いいですね。(3)行きましょう。

田中 ：じゃ、後で連絡しますね。

クマール：わかりました。楽しみにしています。

Expand your conversation

Tanaka ： Kumāru-san, itsu Nihon ni kimashita ka.

Kumāru ： < Kyonen no 9-gatsu > ni kimashita.

....

Tanaka ： (1)Hanami o shita koto ga arimasu ka.

Kumāru ： Iie, arimasen.

Tanaka ： Yokattara, Nichi-yōbi ni (2)issho ni (3)ikimasen ka.

Kumāru ： Ii desu ne. (3)Ikimashō.

Tanaka ： Ja, atode renraku shimasu ne.

Kumāru ： Wakarimashita. Tanoshimi ni shite imasu.

---

①
(1) スノーボードをした   sunō-bōdo o shita
(2) みんなで   minna de
(3) 行き   iki

---

②
(1) 焼酎を飲んだ   shōchū o nonda
(2) 一緒に   issho ni
(3) 飲み   nomi

MEMO

よかったら／yokattara／if you would like to, if it's alright with you

後で連絡します。／atode renraku shimasu.／I will contact you/be in touch later.

楽しみにしています。／Tanoshimi ni shite imasu.／I'm looking forward to it.

みんなで／minna de／with everyone

Listening

Listen to the conversation between the man and woman and choose the correct answer.

Q1   After work

1. They are going to have dinner.
2. They are going out for a drink.
3. They are going home.

Q2   Two co-workers are talking at the office one morning

1. The man asked her out tonight.
2. The man is eating with the woman tonight.
3. The man is eating with the woman tomorrow.

Q3   Two friends are talking

1. The man and woman and no one else are going to see fireworks.
2. The man is going to the fireworks with her.
3. The man is going to see Japanese fireworks by himself.

Q4   Two friends are talking

1. The man is going to see kabuki tonight.
2. The woman has seen kabuki before.
3. They are going to see kabuki on the weekend.

Role playing

Role play using the cards below

A: You want to go see a kabuki performance next month. Ask if B-san has ever seen kabuki, then invite him/her to join you when you go.

B: You have never seen a kabuki before. Accept A-san's invitation.

Do you remember?

Use the phrases you have studied in this unit in situations ①–③ below.

① Would you like to ⋯?

② Have you ever ⋯?

③ Would you like to ⋯ right now?

Phrases for This Unit

Unit Phrases

●お茶を飲みませんか。 ちゃ の	Ocha o nomimasen ka.	Would you like to have a cup of tea?
●温泉に行ったことが おんせん い ありますか。	Onsen ni itta koto ga arimasu ka.	Have you ever been to an onsen (hot spring)?

Useful expressions

●どこに行きましょうか。 い	Doko ni ikimashō ka.	Where shall we go?
●そうしましょう。	Sō shimashō.	Let's do that/it.
●〜はどうですか。	... wa dō desu ka.	How about ...? / How does ... sound?
●〜はちょっと……。	... wa chotto	... is no good for me.
●また誘ってください。 さそ	Mata sasotte kudasai.	Please invite/ ask me again.
●楽しみにしています。 たの	Tanoshimi ni shite imasu.	I'm looking forward to it.

Check!

✓ Now I can...
- ☐ Talk about my own experiences and ask about those of others
- ☐ Invite a person to do or have something
- ☐ Accept and refuse invitations

One More Step

Look at the pictures and talk about events throughout the year.

● Seasonal Event

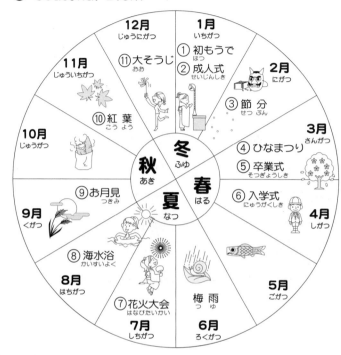

① Hatsumōde / The first visit to a shrine of the new year

② Seijin-shiki / Coming-of-Age, Ceremony for people turning 20

③ Setsubun (Mame-maki) / Ceremony for the end of winter (bean throwing)

④ Hina-matsuri / Girls' Day, the Doll Festival

⑤ Sotsugyō-shiki / School graduations

⑥ Nyūgaku-shiki / Entrance ceremonies

⑦ Hanabi-taikai / Fireworks festivals

⑧ Kaisuiyoku / Sea-bathing

⑨ O-tsukimi / Moon-viewing

⑩ Kōyō / Changing of the leaves

⑪ Ōsōji / Year-end cleaning

do / have done	go / have been	see / have seen
(＿を) します　(＿o) shimasu	(＿に) 行きます　(＿ni) ikimasu	(＿を) 見ます　(＿o) mimasu
→ (＿を) した　(＿o) shita	→ (＿に) 行った　(＿ni) itta	→ (＿を) 見た　(＿o) mita

Talk about the seasonal event like the example below using the verbs above.

(1) 日本では、 <u>４月</u> に <u>入学式</u> をします。

Nihon de wa, <u>4-gatsu</u> ni <u>nyūgaku-shiki</u> o shimasu.

We have entrance ceremonies in April.

→ Explain a tradition in your country*.　　　　*my country = watashi no kuni

(2) <u>初もうで</u> をしたことがありますか。

<u>Hatsumōde</u> o shita koto ga arimasu ka.

Have you ever done *hatsumode*? [the first visit to a shrine of the new year]

→ You can expand the scope of the conversation using the phrases below.

"Doko ni ikimashita ka."(Unit8), "Dō deshita ka."(Unit9), or "Kondo issho ni ikimasen ka."(Unit12)

Grammar | 文 法

| Sentence Structure

1. Basic Sentence Patterns

In broad terms, Japanese sentences can be divided into the following three patterns.

Watashi wa Nihon-jin desu.	I am a Japanese person.	[**Noun Phrase**]
Meari-san wa isogashii desu.	Mary-san is busy.	[**Adjective Phrase**]
Tanaka-san wa rāmen o tabemasu.	Tanaka-san eats ramen.	[**Verb Phrase**]

"**Desu**" has a similar function to "**to be**" in English, and comes at the end of Noun and Adjective Phrases. Verb Phrases end with [**-masu**].

"**Wa**" is a particle that denotes topics and subjects. (The particles "**ga**" and "**mo**" can also indicate a subject. → See p.166 for more information on particles)

2. Negative Sentences

Negative Sentences are made by modifying the end of a predicate, which is typically the last part of a sentence. This grammatical structure is the reason that one must listen to the very end of a Japanese sentence to know whether it is negative or affirmative.

Watashi wa Nihon-jin <u>ja arimasen</u>.	I <u>am not</u> a Japanese person.	[**Negative Noun Phrase**]
Meari-san wa isogashi<u>ku nai desu</u>.	Mary-san <u>is not</u> busy.	[**Negative Adjective Phrase**]
Tanaka-san wa rāmen o tabe<u>masen</u>.	Tanaka-san <u>does not</u> eat ramen.	[**Negative Verb Phrase**]

Please refer to individual chapters for more detailed information on how to make negative sentences using all parts of speech.

3. Interrogative Sentences (Questions)

Attach "**ka**" to the end of a Declarative Sentence to create an Interrogative Sentence.

Meari-san wa isogashii desu <u>ka</u>.	Is Mary-san busy?
Tanaka-san wa rāmen o tabemasu <u>ka</u>.	Does Tanaka-san eat ramen?

→ See p.179 for more information on interrogative words and sentences with wh-words (who, what, when, where, why, and how).

II Particles

Creating longer sentences in Japanese typically involves inserting different kinds of information in between the subject and predicate. Grammatical units known as **"particles"** help simplify this process.

Japanese particles are similar to English prepositions, words like **"in"** and **"at"**. As shown below, while English uses prepositions, which precede the noun, clause, or phrase they modify, Japanese uses postpositions, which come after the clause or phrase.

Kare no <u>heya **de**</u> bangohan o tabemashita.	We had dinner **in** his room.
Maiasa <u>roku-ji **ni**</u> okimasu.	I wake up **at** six o'clock every morning.

Although particles themselves do not carry any meaning, they provide an important role in sentence formation.

For example, English does not use particles and thus relies on word order within a sentence. Changing the order of words in an English sentence can result in a completely different meaning.

I gave <u>her</u> <u>my dog</u>. ≠ *I gave <u>my dog</u> <u>her</u>.

However, what is crucial in a Japanese sentence is not word order, but the units of information made up of a particle and the noun, clause, or phrase it modifies.

Watashi wa <u>kanojo **ni**</u> <u>inu **o**</u> ageta. = Watashi wa <u>inu **o**</u> <u>kanojo **ni**</u> ageta.   (I gave her my dog.)

Even if the words of a sentence appear in a different order, as long as the particles remain the same, the meaning of the sentence does not change.

There are different types of particles. Take a look at the different particles and their functions below.

1. wa

【Subject】

Watashi **wa** Tai-jin desu.	I am a Thai person.
Kore **wa** gohyaku-en desu.	This costs 500 yen.

【Topic】

Kinō **wa** izakaya ni ikimashita.	Yesterday I went to an izakaya.
Natsu-yasumi **wa** nani o shimashita ka.	What did you do over the summer break?

【Comparisons】

Sushi **wa** suki desu ga, sashimi **wa** kirai desu.	I like sushi, but I don't like sashimi.

2. o

【Object】

Shimbun **o** yomimasu.	I read newspapers.
Kōhī **o** nomimasu.	I drink coffee.

3. ni

【Object】

Tomodachi **ni** aimasu.	I'm going to see my friend.
Chichi **ni** nekutai o agemasu.	I'm going to give my dad a necktie.
Basu **ni** norimasu.	I'm going to get on the bus.

【Destination】

Chūgoku **ni** ikimasu.	I'm going to China.
Nihon **ni** kimasu.	I'm coming to Japan.
Uchi **ni** kaerimasu.	I'm going back home.

*The particle **"e"** is used to indicate a general direction as well as a destination, and is interchangeable with **"ni"**.

【Time】

Shichi-ji **ni** okimasu.	I get up at seven o'clock.
Jūichi-ji **ni** nemasu.	I go to bed at eleven o'clock.
San-ji **ni** modorimasu.	I'll come back at three o'clock.

【Location】

Otōto no heya **ni** terebi ga arimasu.	There's a TV in my little brother's room.
Uchi **ni** neko ga imasu.	There's a cat in the house.

4. de

【Place of action】

Resutoran **de** bangohan o tabemasu.	I eat dinner at restaurants.

【Means】

Basu **de** ikimasu.	I'll go by bus.
Hashi **de** tabemasu.	I eat with chopsticks.

【Selection】

- Waiter: Would you like bread or rice? -

Pan **de** onegaishimasu.	Bread, please.

5. no

【Possession】

watashi **no** kuruma	my car
tomodachi **no** hon	my friend's book

【Affiliation】

A-sha **no** shain · an employee of Company A

A-daigaku **no** gakusei · a student at University A

【Attribute (Type/Nature)】

Nihon-go **no** sensei · a teacher of the Japanese language

ichigo **no** shābetto · strawberry sherbet

【Apposition】

tomodachi **no** Yōko-san · my friend, Yoko-san

otto **no** Tomu · my husband, Tom

【Pronoun】

akai **no** · the red one

atsui **no** · the hot one

6. to

【A partner in action】

Tomodachi **to** eiga o mimashita. · I saw a movie with my friend.

Eri-san **to** kekkon shimashita. · I married Eri-san.

Shachō **to** hanashimasu. · I'll talk with the CEO.

【Parallel phrases】

pan **to** tamago · bread and eggs

7. mo

【Sameness/Agreement】

Kore **mo** onegaishimasu. · I'll have this, too, please.

Watashi **mo** eiga ga suki desu. · I also like movies.

【Emphasis】

Wain o go-hon **mo** nomimashita. · I drank five bottles of wine!

8. kara

【Origin of duration or motion】

Uchi **kara** gakkō made samjuppun kakarimasu. · It takes thirty minutes from our house to the school.

9. made

【End of duration or motion】

Ku-ji kara jūichi-ji **made** benkyō shimasu. · I study from nine until eleven o'clock.

10. ga

Although the particle **"ga"** essentially follows the subject of a sentence, it sometimes provides a function similar to other particles. Because this can make **"ga"** confusing to use, try to remember the five patterns below.

【The subject of an interrogative sentence that uses an interrogative word】

Dare **ga** kimasu ka.	Who's coming?
Itsu **ga** ii desu ka.	When would be a good time?

【The subject of a sentence denoting possession or location】

Uchi ni pasokon **ga** arimasu.	We have a computer at our house.
Toire ni neko **ga** imasu.	There's a cat in the restroom.

【The subject of an embedded clause modifying a noun phrase】

Kore wa Bētōben **ga** tsukutta kyoku desu.	This is a piece of music that is composed by Beethoven.

【Objects】 → See p.18

(1) suki, kirai, jōzu, heta   (like, dislike, be good at, be bad at)
   Sakkā **ga** suki desu.   I like soccer.

(2) wakaru, dekiru, mieru, kikoeru   (understand, can do, can see, can hear)
   Koko kara Fuji-san o miru koto **ga** dekimasu.   It is possible to see Mount Fuji from here.

(3) hoshii, shitai   (want, want to do)
   Atarashii terebi **ga** hoshii desu.   I want a new TV.
   Nihon-go **ga** benkyō shitai desu.   I want to study Japanese.

【An aspect of part of the subject】

Imōto wa kami **ga** nagai.	My younger sister has long hair.
Nihon wa hanzai **ga** sukunai.	Japan has little crime.

III Demonstratives

There are four types of Japanese demonstratives, which begin with **"ko-"**, **"so-"**, **"a-"**, and **"do-"** respectively. → See p.28, p.40

The table below shows how they are used.

【Table 1】

Demonstrative	**"ko-"** Close to the speaker	**"so-"** Farther than "ko-" or closer to the listener	**"a-"** Farther than "so-" or far from both the speaker and listener	**"do-"** Which, what, where
S=Speaker L=Listener				
Thing	kore	sore	are	dore
	kono [+noun]	sono [+noun]	ano [+noun]	dono [+noun]
Place	koko	soko	asoko	doko
Direction	kocchi	socchi	acchi	docchi
(Polite)	(kochira)	(sochira)	(achira)	(dochira)
Area	kono hen	sono hen	ano hen	dono hen

IV Existential and Possessive Sentences

An Existential Sentence is a sentence with a phrase describing a location or time in which a noun exists. When the subject of an Existential Sentence is animate (capable of moving), the verb **"imasu/iru"** is used, while **"arimasu/aru"** is used for inanimate objects. → See p.24, p.26, p.38

Kōen ni kodomo ga **imasu**.
Ekimae ni takushī ga **imasu**.
Uchi no mae ni kombini ga **arimasu**.
Niwa ni ki ga **arimasu**.

A little kid is in the park.
Taxis are in front of the station.
There's a convenience store in front of our house.
There's a tree in the garden.

Although a taxi is not alive, because the driver inside is capable of moving, it is consider animate. Likewise, although a tree is a living thing, because it cannot move on its own it is considered inanimate.

"imasu" and **"arimasu"** can also denote possession and scheduling, which are usages derived from their original meaning of existence.

-At a store- Kasa, **arimasu** ka.	Do you have umbrellas?
Ashita kaigi ga **arimasu**.	I have a meeting tomorrow.
Watashi wa imōto ga futari **imasu**.	I have two younger sisters.
Kodomo no koro, uchi ni inu ga **imashita**.	We had a dog at our house when I was a kid.

Although the subject of an Existential Sentence is primarily marked by **"ga"**, there are cases when it is denoted by the topic marker **"wa"**.   → See p.166

V Verbs

Verbs provide a great deal of information in Japanese, including affirmation/negation, tense, and politeness. In broad terms, Japanese verbs can be divided into **polite** and **plain forms**, while Japanese tense is either **past** or **non-past** (used for present and future actions).   → See Unit 8

Although some verbs have irregular conjugations, for the most part they follow the same basic rules.

1. Basic Verb Conjugations and Functions

Polite verbs end in [-masu]. This conjugation is known as either the **masu-form** or the **polite form**.

【Table 2】

Masu-form		Affirmative	Negative
ikimasu Go	Non-past	ikimasu	ikimasen
	Past	ikimashita	Ikimasendeshita

To find a verb in the dictionary, you need to search for the **dictionary form** or the **plain form**.

【Table 3】

Dictionary Form		Affirmative	Negative
taberu Eat	**Non-past**	taberu (dictionary form)	tabenai (nai-form)
	Past	tabeta (ta-form)	tabenakatta

In certain contexts, the **masu-form** and **dictionary form** of a verb are used not to express tense or politeness, but to connect grammatical expressions.

Take a look at what sort of sentences can be made using the **masu-form** and **dictionary form** of the verb "nomu" (drink).

1. Masu-form
nomimasu
+ tai desu (**Desire**)
   Nani ka **nomi**tai desu.   I want something to drink.
+ ni ikimasu (**Destination of motion**)
   Nomi ni ikimasu.   I'm going drinking.

2. Dictionary form
nomu
+ no ga suki desu (**Verb nominalization**)
   Bīru o **nomu** no ga suki desu.   I like drinking beer.
+ koto ga dekimasu (**Verb nominalization**)
   Nihon-shu o **nomu** koto ga dekimasu.   I can drink Japanese sake.

Additional conjugations include the **nai-form**, **ta-form**, and **te-form**.
Let's take a look at what sort of sentences can be made using different forms of the verb "kaku" (write).

3. Nai-form
kakanai
+ nai de kudasai (**Negative request**)
   Koko ni **kaka**nai de kudasai.   Please don't write here/on this.
+ nai to ikemasen (**Obligation**)
   Jūsho mo **kaka**nai to ikemasen.   You must also write down your address.

4. Ta-form   → See Unit 12

kaita

+ koto ga arimasu (**Experience**)

Fan-retā o **kaita** koto ga arimasu.   I've written a fan letter before.

+ hō ga ii desu (**Advice**)

Nihon-go de **kaita** hō ga ii desu.   It'd be better to write it in Japanese.

The **te-form** is considered to be the most essential and crucial of all verb conjugations.

5. Te-form   → See Unit 5, Unit 6

kaite

Te-form (**A request to someone familiar**)

Koko ni namae o **kaite**.   Write your name here.

Te-form (**Verb connector**)

Tegami o **kaite**, neta.   I wrote a letter and went to bed.

+ kudasai (**Request**)

Koko ni namae o **kaite** kudasai.   Please write your name here.

+ imasu (**Progressive action**)

Ima tegami o kaite imasu.   I'm writing a letter right now.

+ mo ii desu ka (**Request for permission**)

Bōrupen de **kaite** mo ii desu ka.   May I write with a ballpoint pen?

2. How to Conjugate Verbs

We will now take a look at each verb conjugation. As mentioned before, although some exceptions do exist, most verbs apart from the two irregular verbs **"suru"** (do) and **"kuru"** (come) conjugate according to the same rules.

Verbs can be divided into three categories according to their conjugations. In order to memorize how verbs conjugate, it is important to first understand these three categories.

1. Ru-verbs

Verbs that end in [-ru] whose final vowel before [-ru] is [i] or [e].

Ex. taberu (eat), miru (look), miseru (show), akeru (open)

*Exceptions: kaeru (go home / return), hairu (enter), hashiru (run), shiru (know) → **u-verb**

2. U-verbs

Verbs that end in sounds beside [ru], such as [u] or [tsu].

Verbs that end in [ru] whose final vowel before [ru] is [a], [u], or [o].

Ex. iku (go), motsu (hold), tobu (fly), sawaru (touch), uru (sell), noru (get on)

3. Irregular verbs

Two verbs, **"suru"** (do) and **"kuru"** (come).

Given the above rules, as long as you are aware of a few exceptions, you can categorize all verbs into one of three groups.

Although **ru-verbs** have the simplest rules for conjugations, the majority of verbs are **u-verbs**.

How to make the dictionary form

1. Ru-verbs

Starting from the **masu-form**, replace [masu] with [ru].

   -masu → **-ru**

   tabemasu → taberu   mimasu → miru

2. U-verbs

Starting from the **masu-form**, remove **[masu]** and replace the final [i] with [u].

   kakimasu → kaku   nomimasu → nomu

Note that sound changes occur when using *kana* from the **sa** and **ta rows**.

   hanashimasu → hanasu   mochimasu → motsu

3. Irregular verbs

   shimasu → suru   kimasu → kuru

How to make the nai-form

1. Ru-verbs

Starting from the **masu-form**, replace [masu] with [nai]

   -masu → **-nai**

   tabemasu → tabenai   mimasu → minai

2. U-verbs

Starting from the **masu-form**, remove [masu] and replace the final [i] with [anai].

   -imasu → **-anai**

   kakimasu → kakanai   nomimasu → nomanai

However, if the final [u] of the **dictionary form** of a verb is preceded by another vowel, the [u] becomes [wa] in the **nai-form**.

   kau → kawanai   iu → iwanai

3. Irregular verbs

shimasu → shinai   kimasu → konai

How to make the te-form

1. Ru-verbs

Starting from the **masu-form**, replace [masu] with [te]

-masu → -te

tabemasu → tabete   mimasu → mite

2. U-verbs

Although creating the **te-forms** of **u-verbs** is slightly complicated, they all obey certain rules, which are determined based on the final speech sound that remains after removing [masu] from the **masu-form** of each verb.

(1) -i, -chi, -ri → -tte

kaimasu → katte   mochimasu → motte   kaerimasu → kaette

(2) -mi, -bi, -ni → -nde

nomimasu → nonde   asobimasu → asonde   shinimasu → shinde

(3) -ki, -gi → -ite, -ide

kakimasu → kaite   oyogimasu → oyoide

*Exception: ikimasu → itte

(4) -shi → -shite

hanashimasu → hanashite

3. Irregular verbs

shimasu → shite   kimasu → kite

*The **ta-form** is identical to the **te-form** conjugation.

VI Adjectives

Like Japanese verbs, Japanese adjectives convey crucial information at the end, such as negation and tense. Two types of Japanese adjectives exist, **i-adjectives** and **na-adjectives**, and they each have their own conjugation pattern.

When attaching an adjective to the front of a noun to create a noun phrase, adjectives that end in [i] are known as **i-adjectives**, and adjectives that end in [na] are called **na-adjectives**.

→ See Unit 9, Unit 10, Unit 11

【Table 4】

I-adjectives	Na-adjectives
hiro**i** heya (a spacious room)	shizuka **na** heya (a quiet room)
furu**i** heya (an old room)	kirei **na** heya (a clean room)

Adjectives function in two ways depending on if they are used in the predicate of a sentence or as part of a noun phrase.

Kono kaban wa **chiisai desu**.	This bag is **small**.
Kore wa **chiisai** kaban desu.	This is a **small** bag.
Kono mondai wa **kantan desu**.	This problem is **simple**.
Kore wa **kantan na** mondai desu.	This is a **simple** problem.

【Table 5】

	I-adjective*1 hiroi (wide)		Na-adjective*2 shizuka (quiet)	
	Affirmative	Negative	Affirmative	Negative
Non-past	hiroi desu	hiro**kunai** desu	shizuka desu	shizuka **dewa/ja arimasen**
Past	hiro**katta** desu	hiro**kunakatta** desu	shizuka **deshita**	shizuka **dewa/ja arimasendeshita**

*1 I-adjective "**ii** (good)" conjugates irregularly.

	Affirmative	Negative
Non-past	ii desu	yokunai desu
Past	yokatta desu	yokunakatta desu

*2 Na-adjectives also include the following conjugation.

	Affirmative	Negative
Non-past	shizuka desu	shizuka janai desu
Past	shizuka datta desu	shizuka janakatta desu

Note that the word [desu] is frequently omitted in casual conversation.

VII Numbers

Japanese has different words for numbers depending on if numbers are said by themselves, or if they are used in conjunction with a counter word.

1. Stand-alone Numbers

Japanese numbers are based around 10, with numbers higher than 10 formed by stating the unit of 10 and then saying the words for 1 through 9.

0 (zero/rei), 1 (ichi), 2 (ni), 3 (san), 4 (yon/shi), 5 (go), 6 (roku), 7 (nana/shichi), 8 (hachi), 9 (kyū/ku), 10 (jū), 11 (jūichi), 12 (jūni), ..., 20 (nijū), ..., 30 (sanjū)

Additionally, individual words exist for units of 10 with additional decimals, ranging from 10 (jū) and 100 (hyaku) to 1,000 (sen) and 10,000 (man). However, numbers higher than these units are composed by combining these four words.

100,000 jūman	1,000,000 hyakuman	10,000,000 (is)senman
100,000,000 (ichi)oku	1,000,000,000,000 (ic)chō	→ See p.47

Stating a phone number: 03-5225-9733 would be [zero san (no) go ni ni go (no) kyū nana san san].

2. Counting time

___ jikan ___hours

1 ichi-jikan	2 ni-jikan	3 san-jikan	4 yo-jikan	5 go-jikan
6 roku-jikan	7 shichi-jikan	8 hachi-jikan	9 ku-jikan	10 jū-jikan
11 jūichi-jikan	12 jūni-jikan	......	20 nijū-jikan	30 sanjū-jikan

___ ji ___o'clock

1 ichi-ji	2 ni-ji	3 san-ji	4 yo-ji	5 go-ji
6 roku-ji	7 shichi-ji	8 hachi-ji	9 ku-ji	10 jū-ji
11 jūichi-ji	12 jūni-ji			

___ fun/pun ___minutes

1 ippun	2 ni-fun	3 sam-pun	4 yon-pun	5 go-fun
6 roppun	7 nana-fun	8 happun	9 kyū-fun	10 juppun
11 jūippun	12 jūni-fun	......	20 nijuppun	30 sanjuppun

Ex. 3:50 = san-ji gojuppun   8:30 = hachi-ji sanjuppun / hachi-ji han (han = half) → See p.103

3. Counters

Japanese uses different counter words depending on what is being counted. → See p.29, p.43, p.53

Uchi ni CD ga hyaku-mai arimasu.	I have 100 CDs at home.
Kuruma ga mō ichi-dai hoshii.	I want one more car.
Hambāgā o futatsu kudasai.	Two hamburgers, please.

Counters are determined by the quality of the object(s) being counted. Numbers have different readings depending on the counter they are used with.

Note that the numbers 1 (ichi), 3 (san), 6 (roku), 8 (hachi), and 10 (jū) are especially prone to change.

【Table 6】

	-mai	-dai	-ko / -tsu	-kai	-hon	-nin
	Flat objects (paper, CDs, DVDs, shirts)	Large inanimate objects (TVs, PCs, cars, bicycles)	Small inanimate objects (eggs, hamburgers, tomatos)	Floors and number of times something is done	Long, tubular objects (pens, umbrellas, bottles)	People
1	ichi-mai	ichi-dai	**ikko/hitotsu**	**ikkai**	**ippon**	**hitori**
2	ni-mai	ni-dai	ni-ko/**futatsu**	ni-kai	ni-hon	**futari**
3	san-mai	san-dai	san-ko/**mittsu**	san-kai*	**sam-bon**	san-nin
4	yon-mai	yon-dai	yon-ko/**yottsu**	yon-kai	yon-hon	**yo-nin**
5	go-mai	go-dai	go-ko/**itsutsu**	go-kai	go-hon	go-nin
6	roku-mai	roku-dai	**rokko/muttsu**	**rokkai**	**roppon**	roku-nin
7	nana-mai	nana-dai	nana-ko/**nanatsu**	nana-kai	nana-hon	shichi-nin
8	hachi-mai	hachi-dai	hachi-ko/**yattsu**	hachi-kai/**hakkai**	hachi-hon/**happon**	hachi-nin
9	kyū-mai	kyū-dai	kyū-ko/**kokonotsu**	kyū-kai	kyū-hon	kyū-nin
10	jū-mai	jū-dai	**jukko/tō**	**jukkai**	**juppon**	jū-nin
?	nam-mai	nan-dai	nan-ko/**ikutsu**	nan-kai*	nam-bon	nan-nin

*When talking about floors of a building, [san-gai] and [nan-gai] are also permissible.

VIII Interrogatives

This section looks at interrogative sentences that use interrogative words like "what" and "who," and provides a lineup of Japanese interrogatives.

Interrogative sentences are usually formed by using an interrogative word for the information you are asking for and adding **"ka"** to the end of the sentence.

1. what = nani / nan

Nani ga suki desu ka.	**What** do you like?
Kore wa **nan** desu ka.	**What** is this? → See Unit 4

2. what time = nan-ji

Nan-ji ni okimasu ka.	**What time** do you wake up?
Shigoto wa **nan-ji** made desu ka.	**What time** do you finish work?

3. where = doko   → See Unit 2, Unit 8

Doko ni ikimasu ka.	**Where** will you go?
Doko de benkyō shimasu ka.	**Where** do you study?

4. who = dare

Dare to ikimasu ka.	**Who** are you going with?
Dare ga kimashita ka.	**Who** came?

When used as the subject of a sentence, interrogative words are always followed by **"ga"**.

5. what + [noun] = nan no + [noun]

Nan no hon o yomimashita ka.	**What book** did you read?

6. what kind of = donna   → See Unit 10

Donna hito desu ka.	**What kind of** person is he/she?
Donna tokoro desu ka.	**What kind of** place is it?

7. how many = nan + [counter] / ikutsu

Nan-jikan benkyō shimashita ka.	**How many hours** did you study?
Nan-nin imasu ka.	**How many people** are there?
Ikutsu arimasu ka.	**How many** are there?

8. how = nan + [counter] / donogurai

Nan-sai desu ka.	**How old** are you?
Donogurai ikimasu ka.	**How often** do you go?
Donogurai tōi desuka.	**How far** is it?
Donogurai kakarimasu ka.	**How long** will it take? → See Unit 7

9. how much = ikura

Ikura desu ka.	**How much** is it? → See Unit 4

10. which = docchi / dochira / dore

with two options	: **Docchi/dochira** ga suki desu ka.	**Which** do you prefer?
with more than two options	: **Dore** ga (ichiban) suki desu ka.	**Which** do you like [the most]?

IX Adverbs

In Japanese, adverbs come before verbs and adjectives and describe their state or degree.

【State adverbs】

Yukkuri hanashite kudasai.	Please talk **slowly**.
Kono machi wa **sukkari** kawatta.	This town has **completely** changed.
Kichinto setsumei shite kudasai.	Please explain this **precisely**.

【Degree adverbs】

Totemo oishii desu.	It's **very** delicious.
Nihon-go to Eigo wa **kanari** chigau.	Japanese and English are **pretty** different.
Itsumo wa bīru desu ga, **tamani** shōchū o nomimasu.	
	I **always** drink beer, but **sometimes** I'll have shochu.
Eiga wa **amari** suki ja arimasen.	I do**n't really** like movies.
Watashi wa kanojo o **zenzen** shiranai.	I do**n't** know her **at all**.

Affirmative adverbs include **"totemo"** and **"kanari"** that describe degree and others like **"itsumo"** and **"tamani"** that describe frequency. Negative adverbs include **"amari"** and **"zenzen"**.

Some adjectives like the ones listed below can be conjugated to function as adverbs.

hayai	→	hayaku	**Hayaku** tsukimashita.	I arrived **early**.
osoi	→	osoku	**Osoku** okimashita.	I woke up **late**.
sugoi	→	sugoku	Fuji-san wa **sugoku** kirei da.	Mt. Fuji is **amazingly** beautiful.
shizuka **na**	→	shizuka **ni**	**Shizuka ni** aruite kudasai.	Please walk **quietly**.
pojithibu **na**	→	pojithibu **ni**	Motto **pojithibu ni** kangaeyou.	Let's think more **positively**.

X Omitting words

Particularly in spoken conversation, certain parts of a Japanese sentence can be omitted. Consider the examples below.

1. Subject omission

(Watashi wa) Jon desu.	(I am) John.	
(Watashi wa) kaishain desu.	(I am) a company employee.	
(Watashi wa) Amerika kara kimashita.	(I am) from the United States.	→ See Unit 1

Subjects that can be quickly understood from context in both interrogative and declarative sentences, particularly in ones in which the listener is the subject, are frequently omitted.

It is important to note that the word **"anata"**, which corresponds to the word **"you"** in English, is hardly ever used in Japanese conversation. Instead, a person's name or job title is used when it is necessary to explicitly refer to them in conversation.

(Anata wa) kaishain desu ka.	(Are you) a company employee?
(Tanaka-san,) ima, isogashii desu ka.	(Tanaka-san, are you) busy right now?
(Sensei wa) rāmen o tabe masu ka.	(Sensei, do you) eat ramen?

2. Interrogative omission

When asking a question using an interrogative word in conversation, there are also times when the question word itself is omitted and only the subject is uttered.

O-shigoto wa (nan desu ka)?	What do you do?	
O-namae wa (nan desu ka)?	What is your name?	→ See Unit 1

Like **"anata"**(you), the phrase **"anata no"**(your) is also not used when it can be easily inferred from context.

XI Respectful Language

All languages have a method of conveying politeness depending on who someone is speaking to. Japanese is no exception to this, and Japanese keigo, or respectful language, is divided into two categories depending on who is speaking to whom. Sonkei-go, or honorific language, is used to promote the stature of a respectable person (listener or third party), while kenjō-go, or humble language, is used to lower the speaker's own status. The **desu/masu-form** is sometimes referred to as teinei-go, or polite language, which can be considered a form of keigo, but unlike sonkei-go and kenjō-go, both listener and speaker can use the **desu/masu-form** to show respect.

For example, the verb **"taberu"** (eat) has completely different forms depending on whether it is in teinei-go (polite), sonkei-go (honorific), or kenjō-go (humble).

Ex.1   **Taberu** (eat)

Teinei-go	tabemasu
Sonkei-go	meshiagarimasu
Kenjō-go	itadakimasu

While some verbs like **"taberu"** are replaced with completely different words when using polite language, most verbs follow a simple rule to promote the listener (**o+[masu-form stem]+ni narimasu**) or to demote the speaker (**o+[masu-form stem]+shimasu**). Additionally, attaching **[-rareru]** or **[-areru]** to the stem of a **ru-verb** or **u-verb**, respectively, can also be used to promote the listener.

Ex. 2   **Kariru** (borrow)

Teinei-go	karimasu
Sonkei-go	okari ni narimasu / kariraremasu
Kenjō-go	okarishimasu

Ex. 3

- A-san is a librarian at a museum reference room. B-san is a student. -

A: Kono shiryō, okari ni narimasu ka / kariraremasu ka.

B: Ee, okari shitai desu.

A: Would you like to borrow these materials?

B: Yes, I would [like to borrow them].

Keigo is not only limited to verbs. Nouns can be modified with bika-go, or beautified language, to show respect.
In bika-go, the prefix **"o"** or **"go"** is attached to a noun.

Ex. o-mizu (water), o-sara (plate), o-hashi (chopsticks)
    go-shusshin (hometown), go-kazoku (family), go-shumi (hobby)

"o" is attached to wago, or native Japanese words, while **"go"** is attached to kango, or words that were borrowed from Chinese.

Keigo is often found in phrases frequently used at places that serve customers, such as shops, facilities, and areas of public transport. Sonkei-go phrases that elevate the status of the customer include "Omachi kudasai." (Please wait.), "Yukkuri goran ni natte kudasai." (Please take your time and have a look.), and "Irasshaimase." (Welcome.)
Kenjō-go phrases that workers use to demote their own status include "Omatase shimashita." (Thank you for waiting.), "Sugu omochi shimasu." (I'll bring that right out.), and "Densha ga mairimasu." (A train is coming.), which can be heard all across Japan.

While the above was a brief introduction to Japanese polite language, keigo is not limited to verbs. Politeness in the Japanese language is an expansive system that extends all the way to nouns and adjectives, and reflects the dynamic between the people who use it and the people to whom it is used. Because of this complexity, keigo is not an aspect of the Japanese language that Japanese people naturally acquire and use without thinking, but a system that must be consciously studied.
Although it may take time for students of Japanese to comfortably use keigo, opportunities to listen to polite language abound at restaurants, buses, trains, and a variety of public places, so please begin your studies by listening to the keigo around you.

Translation of Dialogue

p.20 UNIT 1

John   : How do you do. I'm John. It's nice to meet you.

Tanaka : How do you do. I'm Tanaka. The pleasure is all mine. John-san, what country are you from?

John   : The United States.

Tanaka : I see. And where do you live?

John   : In Chiba. How about you?

Tanaka : I live in Nakano. Do you like Japanese food?

John   : Yes, I like tempura. / No, not really.

Tanaka : Oh, OK.

p.32 UNIT 2

Kumar : Excuse me.

Woman : Yes?

Kumar : I'm trying to get to Sakura Park.

Woman : It's straight down this way.

Kumar : Okay. Oh, also, is there an ATM near here?

Woman : Let me think.... There's a convenience store.

Kumar : Where is the convenience store?

Woman : In front of Sakura Park.

Kumar : Thank you.

p.46 UNIT 3

John   : Excuse me, do you have T-shirts?

Clerk   : Yes, we do. They're right here.

John   : How much does that cost?

Clerk   : It's 3900 yen.

John   : Do you have anything a little cheaper?

Clerk   : This one is 1980 yen.

John   : OK, then I'll take three of those.

Clerk   : Thank you.

p.60 UNIT 4

Waitress : Are you ready to order?

John   : What do you recommend?

Waitress : Today's lunch.

John   : Then, I'll have one of those, please.

Waitress : What would you like to drink?

John   : Cola, please.

Waitress : Would you like dessert with that?

John   : No, thank you.

- During the meal -

John   : Excuse me, could I have some water?

Waitress : Right away.

p.72 UNIT 5

John   : Excuse me, I'd like to become a member.

Clerk : Do you have any ID on you today?

John   : Would you accept the alien registration card?

Clerk : Yes, that's alright. Also do you have a picture?

John   : Um, can I bring one next time?

Clerk : No problem. Please fill this out, then.

John   : Can I borrow this pen?

Clerk : Yes, please.

p.86 UNIT 6

John   : Oh, Tanaka-san. Please have a seat.

Tanaka : Thank you.

John   : Have something to drink.

Tanaka : Ah, thanks.

John   : Should I get you some chopsticks?

Tanaka : I have some so it's okay.

- Later -

John   : Excuse me, Tanaka-san, could you pass me the salt?

Tanaka : Here you go.

p.98 UNIT 7

John : How do I get from Tokyo to Kyoto?

Suzuki : By bus or Shinkasen.

John : How long does it take by bus?

Suzuki : About six hours.

John : How much does it cost?

Suzuki : I think it's about 7,000 yen.

John : I see. Thank you.

p.112 UNIT 8

Tanaka : John-san, what did you do on the weekend?

John : I went out to eat in Shinjuku. What about you, Tanaka-san?

Tanaka : I had a relaxing time at home. What are you going to do on your next day off?

John : I'm going to the park with my children.

Tanaka : What will you do there?

John : I want to take pictures.

Tanaka : That sounds nice.

p.124 UNIT 9

Sato : How was last weekend?

Karen : It was very fun! It was my first visit to Kyoto. Kyoto is a very nice town.

Sato : I see. How do you like Japanese temples?

Karen : They're very beautiful.

p.138 UNIT 10

John : What does nikujaga taste like?

Suzuki : It's sweet. It's really good.

John : Okay.
This looks spicy, doesn't it?

Suzuki : Yes, it does.

John : I see. I'm not too good with spicy food. I can't eat it.

Suzuki : Well, let's get something else. How about this?

John : That looks good.

Suzuki : Then let's have this.

p.150 UNIT 11

Tanaka : Hello. It sure is cold today.

Kumar : It really is. How has your job been lately?

Tanaka : It's been well. How about your job, Kumar-san?

Kumar : I've been busy.

- Later -

Kumar : If you'll excuse me, I need to be going home.

Tanaka : Alright. Take care.

Kumar : See you later.

p.160 UNIT 12

Tanaka : Kumar-san, when did you come to Japan?

Kumar : Last September.

Tanaka : Have you ever gone flower-viewing?

Kumar : No, I haven't.

Tanaka : If you're interested, would you like to go flower-viewing together on Sunday?

Kumar : That sounds great. I'd like to.

Tanaka : Okay. I'll be in touch later.

Kumar : Alright. I'm looking forward to it.

Listening Answers and CD Script

p.21 **[UNIT 1] Q1** 1 **Q2** 3 **Q3** 1 **Q4** 3

Q1

M: Hajimemashite. Watashi wa Tomu desu.
   Igirisu-jin desu. Dōzo yoroshiku.
F: Emiri desu. Ōsutoraria kara kimashita.
   Kochira koso, dōzo yoroshiku.

M: How do you do. I'm Tom. I'm English.
   It's nice to meet you.
F: I'm Emily. I'm from Australia.
   The pleasure is mine.

Q2

F: Nīru-san, go-shusshin wa?
M: Indo desu.
F: O-shigoto wa nan desu ka.
M: Kaishain desu.

F: Neal-san, where are you from?
M: India.
F: What do you do?
M: I work for a company.

Q3

M: Ueda-san, karaoke wa suki desu ka.
F: Ūn, watashi wa amari….
   Demo, ongaku wa suki desu yo.

M: Ueda-san, do you like karaoke?
F: Well…, not so much. But I do like music.

Q4

F: Tomu-san, o-sake wa suki desu ka.
M: Hai, suki desu. Bīru ga suki desu.
   Yamada-san mo o-sake, suki desu ka.
F: Ee, watashi mo suki desu yo.

F: Tom-san, do you like drinking?
M: Yes, I do. I like beer. Do you drink, too?
F: Yes, I sure do.

p.34 **[UNIT 2] Q1** 1 **Q2** 2 **Q3** 1 **Q4** 2

Q1

M: Sumimasen. Kono hen ni intanetto-kafe,
   arimasu ka.
F: Ee, asoko ni arimasu yo.
M: Arigatō gozaimasu.
F: Dō itashimashite.

M: Excuse me. Is there an internet café around
   here?
F: Yes, it's over there.
M: Thank you.
F: You're welcome.

Q2

F: Sumimasen, reji, doko desu ka.
M: Achira ni narimasu.
F: A, arigatō gozaimasu.

F: Excuse me, where is the cash register?
M: It's over there.
F: Ah, thank you.

Q3

M: Ano…, hon-ya wa nan-kai desu ka.
F: 3-kai ni narimasu.
M: E, mō ichido ii desu ka.
F: 3-kai desu.
M: Arigatō gozaimasu.

M: Um…, what floor is the bookstore on?
F: The third floor.
M: Pardon? Could you say that one more time?
F: It's on the third floor.
M: Thank you.

Q4

M: Sumimasen,100-en shoppu ni ikitai n desu ga
   ….
F: A, mukō. Ano kombini no ushiro ni arimasu yo.
M: Arigatō gozaimasu.

M: Excuse me, I'm trying to get to the 100-yen
   store, but….
F: Ah, it's over there. It's behind that convenience
   store.
M: Thank you.

p.48 **[UNIT 3] Q1** 3 **Q2** 2 **Q3** 2 **Q4** 1

Q1

M: Sumimasen, tabako arimasu ka.
F: Mōshiwake arimasen. Tabako wa nai n desu.
M: A, sō desu ka. Wakarimashita.

M: Excuse me, do you have cigarettes?
F: I'm sorry, but we don't.
M: Oh, I see.

186

Q2

M: Sumimasen, kore, ikura desu ka.
F: Kasa wa…, 600-en desu.
M: Kono chizu wa ikura desu ka.
F: Sore wa 800-en desu.
M: A, wakarimashita.

M: Excuse me, how much is this?
F: Umbrellas are... 600 yen.
M: How much is this map?
F: That's 800 yen.
M: Oh, okay.

Q3

M: Sumimasen, o-bentō arimasu ka.
F: Hai, kochira desu.
M: Jā, sore futatsu kudasai.
F: Kashikomarimashita.

M: Excuse me, do you have bento boxes?
F: Yes, they're right here.
M: Okay, then I'll have two, please.
F: Right away.

Q4

M: Irasshaimase.
F: Sumimasen, kore, mōchotto ōkii no, arimasen ka.
M: Mōshiwake arimasen. Kore dake nandesu.
F: A, wakarimashita.

M: Welcome
F: Excuse me, do you have a bigger one of these?
M: I'm sorry, but that's all we have.
F: Oh, I see.

p.62 **[UNIT 4] Q1** 3 **Q2** 1 **Q3** 1 **Q4** 2

Q1

M: Go-chūmon okimari desu ka.
F: Osusume wa nan desu ka.
M: Ikura desu.
F: Ikura tte nan desu ka.
M: Kochira desu. Sāmon-eggu desu yo.
F: Ā, jā, sore hitotsu kudasai.

M: Are you ready to order?
F: What do you recommend?
M: *Ikura*.
F: What is *ikura*?
M: This. It's salmon eggs.
F: Ooooh. OK, then I'll have one of those, please.

Q2

F: Irasshaimase. Kochira de omeshiagari desu ka.
M: Hai, koko de.
F: Go-chūmon o dōzo.
M: Chīzu-bāgā to aisu-kōhī onegaishimasu.
F: Kashikomarimashita. Gamu-shiroppu to miruku wa go-riyō desu ka.
M: A, gamu-shiroppu wa, kekkō desu.

F: Welcome. Will you be eating here?
M: Yes.
F: Please order when you are ready.
M: I'll have a cheeseburger and an iced coffee, please.
F: Okay. Would you like cream and liquid sugar?
M: Ah, no liquid sugar, thank you.

Q3

M: O-nomimono wa ikaga desu ka.
F: Jā, kore to onaji no o onegaishimasu.
M: Hai, nama-bīru o o-hitotsu desu ne.
F: Hai.

M: Would you like something (else) to drink?
F: I'll have another one of this.
M: Okay, so one more draft beer, then.
F: Thank you.

Q4

F: Arigatō gozaimashita. O-kaikei wa go-issho de yoroshii desu ka.
M: A, betsubetsu de.
F: Reshīto wa?
M: Kekkō desu.

F: Thank you. Will you be paying together?
M: Um, separate please.
F: Do you need a receipt?
M: No, thank you.

p.74 **[UNIT 5] Q1** 1 **Q2** 3 **Q3** 2 **Q4** 2

Q1

M: Sumimasen, koko, tabako o sutte mo ii desu ka.
F: Mōshiwake gozaimasen. Kochira wa kin'en-seki nandesu.
M: Wakarimashita.

M: Excuse me, but can I smoke here?
F: I'm terribly sorry, but these are non-smoking seats.
M: I see.

Q2

M: Anō, kore, moratte mo ii desu ka.
F: Panfuretto desu ne. Ii desu yo. Sampuru mo dōzo.
M: A, dōmo.

M: Um, could I take one of these?
F: You must mean the pamphlets. That's fine. Here's a free sample for you, too.
M: Ah, thanks.

Q3

F: Kochira ni go-kinyū kudasai.
M: Rōma-ji de ii desu ka.
F: Ee, kekkō desu.

F: Please fill this out.
M: Can I write in Roman letters?
F: Yes, that's fine.

Q4

M: 710-en ni narimasu.
F: Sumimasen, ichiman-en satsu de ii desu ka.
M: Ēto, a, daijōbu desu yo.
F: Jā, kore de.
M: Hai, arigatō gozaimashita.

M: That comes to 710 yen.
F: I'm sorry, but could I pay with a 10,000-yen note?
M: Hmm... ah, yes, that's fine.
F: Alright, then out of this, please.
M: Right away.

p.87 **[UNIT 6] Q1** 1 **Q2** 3 **Q3** 1 **Q4** 2

Q1

F: Sumimasen, kasa o kashite moraemasen ka.
M: Kochira de yoroshii desu ka.
F: Hai, arigatō gozaimasu.

F: Excuse me, but would you lend me an umbrella?
M: Is this one okay?
F: Yes, thank you.

Q2

F: Okimari desu ka.
M: Sumimasen, chotto matte kudasai.
F: Hai, kashikomarimashita.

F: Are you ready to order?
M: I'm sorry, could I have a minute?
F: Yes, sir.

Q3

M: Koko massugu desu ka.
F: A, iie. Shingō o hidari ni magatte kudasai.
M: Hai.

M: It's straight down here?
F: Ah, no. Please turn left at the traffic light.
M: Okay.

Q4

M: Anō, kono wain, nonde mo ii desu ka.
F: Dōzo, dōzo.
M: A, sumimasen. Sono gurasu, totte moraemasen ka.

M: Can I drink this wine?
F: Yes, yes, please.
M: Ah, thank you. Could you pass me that glass?

p.100 **[UNIT 7] Q1** 2 **Q2** 2 **Q3** 3 **Q4** 2

Q1

F: Sumimasen, kore, Hakone ni ikimasu ka.
M: Iie, Hakone wa tsugi no densha desu yo.
F: Arigatō gozaimasu.

F: Excuse me, does this (train) go to Hakone?
M: No, for Hakone you need the next train.
F: Thank you.

Q2

F: Sumimasen, Roppongi-hiruzu made dōyatte ikeba ii desu ka.
M: Chikatetsu de norikae ka…, asoko kara basu de ippon desu ne.
F: A, sō desu ka. Dōmo.

F: Excuse me, how do you get to Roppongi Hills?
M: You can transfer in the subway, or... you can go straight there with the bus over there.
F: Oh, I see. Thank you.

Q3

M: Sumimasen, koko kara Tōkyō-dōmu made doyatte ikeba ii desu ka.
F: Basu ka densha desu ne.
M: Densha de donogurai kakarimasu ka.
F: 10-pun gurai desu yo.
M: A, sō desu ka. Arigatō gozaimasu.

M: Excuse me, how do you get to Tokyo Dome from here?
F: You can take a bus or a train.
M: How long would a train take?

F: About 10 minutes.
M: Oh, I see. Thank you.

Q4
M: Nakamura-san, Tōkyō kara Ōsaka made donogurai kakarimasu ka.
F: Hikōki de1-jikan gurai desu yo.
M: Jā, shinkansen wa?
F: Shinkansen de wa 3-jikan gurai desu yo.

M: Nakamura-san, how far is it from Tokyo to Osaka?
F: It's about an hour by plane.
M: What about by Shinkansen?
F: That's about three hours.

p.113 [UNIT 8] Q1 3 Q2 1 Q3 1 Q4 2

Q1
M: Otsukaresama desu
F: Otsukaresama.
M: Korekara doko ni ikimasu ka.
F: Korekara hon-ya ni ikimasu. Ota-san wa?
M: Boku wa korekara, tomodachi to gohan o tabe ni ikimasu.
F: He, ii desu ne.

M: Hey.
F: Hello.
M: Where are you going now?
F: I'm going to the bookstore. How about you?
M: I'm going to get something to eat with a friend.
F: Oh, that sounds nice.

Q2
F: Ohayō gozaimasu.
M: Ohayō gozaimasu.
F: Shūmatsu, nani o shimashita ka.
M: Shūmatsu wa shigoto deshita.
F: Sō desu ka.
M: Yamada-san wa?
F: Watashi wa kōen ni ikimashita yo. Kazoku to.
M: Hē, ii desu ne.

F: Good morning.
M: Good morning!
F: What'd you do on the weekend?
M: My weekend was work....
F: Really....
M: What about you, Yamada-san?
F: I went to the park, with my family.
M: Oh, that sounds nice.

Q3
M: Natsu-yasumi, nani o shimasu ka.
F: Umi ni ikitai desu. Takahashi-san wa?
M: Watashi wa uchi de yukkuri shitai desu. Demo, umi mo ii desu ne.
F: Jā, issho ni ikimashō.
M: Ii desu ne. Ikimashō.

M: What are you doing for the summer break?
F: I'm going to the beach. What about you, Takahashi-san?
M: I just want to relax at home. But the beach sounds nice.
F: We should go together!
M: That sounds great. Let's do it!

Q4
F: Tomu-san, shūmatsu, nani o shimashita ka.
M: Nihon-go o benkyō shimashita.
F: Sō desu ka. Uchi de?
M: Iie, gakkō de.
F: Hē, kondo no yasumi mo gakkō desu ka.
M: Iie, dokoka asobi ni ikitai desu.
F: Sō desu ka.

F: Tom-san, what did you do on the weekend?
M: I studied Japanese.
F: I see. At home?
M: No, at school.
F: Really! Are you going back to school on your next day off?
M: No, I'm going to go have fun somewhere.
F: I see.

p.126 [UNIT 9] Q1 1 Q2 2 Q3 3 Q4 1

Q1
M: An-san, Nihon no seikatsu wa dō desu ka.
F: Sugoku omoshiroi desu.
M: Sore wa yokatta. Ima sundeiru tokoro wa dō desu ka.
F: Un, totemo kirei desu yo. Demo, chotto takai desu.
M: Sō desu ne. Tōkyō wa takai desu yo ne.

M: Ann-san, how do you like living in Japan?
F: It's so much fun here.
M: I'm happy to hear that. How is where you're living right now?
F: Oh yes, it's very fun. Although a little expensive ....
M: I'll bet. Tokyo sure is expensive, isn't it?

Q2

M: Hayashi-san, kinō no nomikai wa dō deshita ka.
F: Māmā deshita. A, demo ryōri wa oishikatta desu yo.
M: A, sō desu ka.

M: Hayashi-san, how was yesterday's drinking party?
F: It was alright. Oh, but the food was delicious.
M: Oh really?

Q3

F: Ueda-san, ryokō wa dō deshita ka.
M: Taihen deshita. Totemo isogashikatta desu.
F: Sō desu ka. Hoteru wa dō deshita ka.
M: Ā, hoteru wa yokatta desu yo.
F: Sore wa yokatta desu ne.

F: Ueda-san, how was your trip?
M: It was terrible. I was so busy.
F: Really? How was the hotel?
M: Oh, the hotel was nice.
F: Well, I'm glad to hear that.

Q4

F: Maikeru-san, yasumi wa dō deshita ka.
M: Tanoshikatta desu. Tomodachi to Kyōto no o-tera ni ikimashita.
F: Sō desu ka. Ii desu ne. Nihon no o-tera wa dō desu ka.
M: Totemo kirei desu. Subarashii desu.

F: Michael-san, how was your vacation?
M: It was fun. I went with a friend to some temples in Kyoto.
F: Did you? That sounds nice. How do you like Japanese temples?
M: They're so beautiful. They're wonderful.

p.139 **[UNIT 10] Q1** 3 **Q2** 2 **Q3** 3 **Q4** 2

Q1

F: Kimu-san, kore, tabete mimasu ka.
M: Sore, donna aji desu ka.
F: Chotto suppai desu yo. Demo, oishii desu yo.
M: Jā, tabete mimasu.

F: Kim-san, why don't you try this?
M: What does it taste like?
F: It's a little sour. But it's good!
M: Okay, I'll give it a try.

Q2

M: Saitō-san, are, oishisō desu ne. Nan desu ka.
F: Ā, are wa, shabu-shabu desu yo. Gyūniku desu.
M: Ā, gyūniku desu ka.
F: Nigate desu ka.
M: Ee, chotto…. Nigate nandesu.

M: Saito-san, that sure looks good. What is it?
F: Oh, that's shabu-shabu. With beef.
M: Oh, beef?
F: Do you not like beef?
M: Yeah, I don't really eat it.

Q3

F: Nan ni shimasu ka. Kore wa dō desu ka.
M: Kore, nan desu ka.
F: Tōfu to shīfūdo no sarada desu.
M: Hē, karada ni yosasō desu ne. Jā, kore ni shimashō.

F: What will you have? How about this?
M: What is it?
F: It's a tofu and seafood salad.
M: Wow, that sounds healthy. I'll have that, then.

Q4

M: Kimuchi wa dō desu ka.
F: Kimuchi? Kimuchi tte, donna aji desu ka.
M: Karai desu yo. Demo, oishii desu.
F: Ā, karai mono wa chotto….
M: Sō desu ka. Jā, hoka no ni shimashō.

M: How about kimchi?
F: Kimchi? What does kimchi taste like?
M: It's spicy, but it tastes really good.
F: Oh, I'm not so good with spicy foods.
M: Oh yeah? Then let's have something else.

p.151 **[UNIT 11] Q1** 3 **Q2** 1 **Q3** 1 **Q4** 2

Q1

F: A, dōmo. Kyō mo ii tenki desu ne.
M: Sō desu ne. Mainichi atatakai desu ne.
F: Hontō desu ne.
M: Jā, ittekimasu.
F: Itterasshai.

F: Hello. We have nice weather today, too, don't we?
M: Yes, it's been warm everyday, hasn't it?
F: It really has.
M: Well, I'm off.

F: Have a nice day.

Q2

F: Konnichiwa. Saikin, chōshi wa dō desu ka.
M: Okagesama de, genki desu. Yamada-san wa?
F: Watashi mo genki desu. Demo, shigoto ga isogashikute….
M: Taihen desu ne.

F: Hello. How have you been lately?
M: I've been OK, knock on wood. How about you?
F: I've been good, too. But work sure is busy….
M: It's rough, isn't it?

Q3

F: Sumimasen, sorosoro kaerimasu. O-saki ni shitsurei shimasu.
M: Otsukaresama deshita. Ki o tsukete.
F: Jā, mata raishū.

F: Excuse me, but I'm heading home. I'll see you later.
M: Good work today. Take care.
F: See you next week.

Q4

F: Konnichiwa. O-hisashiburi desu ne.
M: O-hisashiburi desu, Yamada-san.
F: O-genki desu ka.
M: Okagesama de. Kyō wa kaze ga tsuyoi desu ne,
F: Hontō. Samui desu ne.

F: Hello! It certainly has been a while.
M: It really has, Yamada-san.
F: How are you doing?
M: I'm good, fortunately. The wind is really strong today, isn't it?
F: I know! It's so cold.

p.161 [UNIT 12] Q1 2 Q2 1 Q3 2 Q4 3

Q1

M: Otsukaresama. Emiri-san, korekara issho ni nomi ni ikimasen ka.
F: Ii desu ne. Doko ni ikimashō ka.
M: Shibuya wa dō desu ka.
F: Un, sō shimashō.

M: Hey there, Emily-san. Would you want to go get a drink together?
F: That sounds great. Where should we go?

M: How does Shibuya sound?
F: Great, let's do it.

Q2

F: Ohayō gozaimasu.
M: Ohayō gozaimasu. A, Yamada-san, komban issho ni gohan o tabe ni ikimasen ka.
F: Sumimasen. Komban wa chotto….
M: Sō desu ka. Jā, mata kondo.
F: Sumimasen, mata sasotte kudasai.

F: Good morning.
M: Good morning. Oh, Yamada-san, would you like to get something to eat tonight?
F: I'm sorry, but tonight's not so good.
M: It's not? Well, next time, then.
F: Sorry about that. Do ask me again, though.

Q3

F: Tomu-san, Nihon no hanabi o mita koto ga arimasu ka.
M: Hanabi? Iie, mada desu.
F: Yokattara, shūmatsu minna de hanabi o mimasen ka.
M: Ii desu ne.
F: Jā, atode renraku shimasu ne.

F: Tom-san, have you ever seen fireworks in Japan?
M: Fireworks? No, not yet.
F: If you can, would you want to come see fireworks with everyone this weekend?
M: I sure would!
F: Okay, I'll get in touch with you later.

Q4

M: Natari-san, kabuki o mita koto ga arimasu ka.
F: Iie, arimasen.
M: Shūmatsu, issho ni ikimasen ka.
F: Ii desu ne. Ikimashō.

M: Natalie-san, have you ever seen kabuki?
F: No, I haven't.
M: Would you want to go this weekend?
F: That sounds great. Let's do it.

● 著者紹介 ●

緒方 由希子　OGATA Yukiko

いいだばし日本語学院講師。静岡県出身。美大卒業後、DTP、帽子デザインなどの仕事に携わる。日本語教師という職業を知り、異文化交流に興味があったことから日本語教師に転向。現在は駿台外語綜合学院、ボランティア教室での講師も。

角谷 佳奈　SUMITANI Kana

いいだばし日本語学院スタッフ兼講師。学習者ニーズ調査やカウンセリング担当。千葉県出身。大学で日本文学・日本語学専攻。通信会社勤務、速記者、ボランティア日本語教師経験後、現職に。海外一人旅にて様々なコミュニケーション術を学ぶ。

左 弥寿子　HIDARI Yasuko

いいだばし日本語学院スタッフ兼講師。教材・カリキュラム開発担当。海産物卸売業を営む両親のもと、長崎に生まれる。スコットランドの大学院にて「産業としてのロック音楽」を研究。文化関連のシンクタンク勤務を経て、現職。

渡部 由紀子　WATANABE Yukiko

いいだばし日本語学院代表。タイでの日本語教育、㈱リクルートでの営業職を経て、ボランティア日本語グループWAIWAIで代表を務めるなど10年間活動。いいだばし日本語学院を設立し、会話中心の少人数レッスンで多様な学習ニーズに応えられるサービスを目指す。2児の母。

著者連絡先 : info@funjapanese.net
制作ご協力者 : Steve Kingさん、大場麻佐代さん、左 江里子さん、左 文江さん、駒場整骨院の先生、Matthew Harveyさん、渡部実亜さん、角谷収さん、白戸直人さん、Anahita Riaziさん、桜井愛子さん他いいだばし日本語学院スタッフ

NIHONGO FUN & EASY　Survival Japanese Conversation for Beginners

2009年12月11日	初版第1刷発行
著者	緒方由希子、角谷佳奈、左 弥寿子、渡部由紀子
DTP	鮫島幹夫
翻訳	Ben Milam
イラスト	平塚徳明
装丁・本文デザイン	吉田清美 [アスク出版]
写真提供協力	ラーメン専門 三代目 月見軒
ナレーション	Jason Hancock、廣瀬和也、深山信嗣、緒方由希子、角谷佳奈、左 弥寿子
録音	株式会社巧芸創作
CDプレス	メモリーテック株式会社
発行	株式会社アスクインターナショナル
	〒162-8558　東京都新宿区下宮比町2-6　　電話: 03-3267-6862
発売	株式会社アスク出版
	〒162-8558　東京都新宿区下宮比町2-6　　電話: 03-3267-6864
発行人	天谷修身
印刷・製本	株式会社光邦
ISBN	978-4-87217-721-3　　©OGATA Yukiko, SUMITANI Kana, HIDARI Yasuko, WATANABE Yukiko